·COMPUTER CLUB·

VOLCANOES

Text:
Hilary Knight & David Wright

Programs:
Dr David Burgess

Macdonald

A MACDONALD BOOK

© Macdonald & Co (Publishers) 1985

First published in 1985
by Macdonald & Co (Publishers) Ltd
London & Sydney
A BPCC plc Company

ISBN 0 356 11022 2

Printed and bound in Belgium
by Henri Proost

Macdonald & Co (Publishers) Ltd
Maxwell House
Worship Street
London EC2A 2EN

Series Editor
Daphne Butler

Book Editors
Donna Bailey
Daphne Butler

Production
Rosemary Bishop

Picture Research
Caroline Mitchell

Consultants
Derrick Daines
Ian Mercer

Teacher Panel
Wendy Cunningham
Debbie Twineham

Design Concept
Sally Henry

Book Design
Richard Garratt

Illustrators
Robert Burns
Gary Hincks
Brian Watson
Paula Youens

Photographs
British Geological Survey 8, 9, 38(*b*), 39(*b*)
BTA 26-27
GeoScience Features 14(*b*), 15, 38(*t*)
Historic Newspaper Service 24
Rex Features 14(*t*), 25(*b*)
Solarfilma, 11, 16, 43
U.S. Geological Survey 4
Ward's 5
ZEFA 7, 8(*b*), 17, 20, 25(*t*), 26, 27, 28, 39(*t*)

British library cataloguing data
Knight, Hilary
    Volcanoes.—(Computer club)
    1. Volcanoes—Juvenile literature
    I. Title II. Wright, David III. Series
    551.2′1   QE521.3

ISBN 0-356-11022-2

About this book

There are three different ways in which you can use this book. One way is to use it to find out more about volcanoes. A second way is to use the programs and information to carry out volcano projects with a microcomputer. The third way is to use the programs to develop your computer skills. Projects for the computer are on pages with a blue border. Each project is positioned in the book next to volcano information needed for the program.

About the programs

The programs are written in structured BASIC for the BBC microcomputer, and are designed to be changed and adapted. Each project page has a description of the program, a listing of the program, and suggestions for changes you can make.

Start by reading the description and then type the program in at the keyboard of your computer. The program must be copied exactly. It is very likely that you will make mistakes and before the program will run it must be debugged.

When the program is running properly you can use it as part of a volcano project. You can also try out the program changes suggested after the program listing. Perhaps you can invent your own modifications.

The programs can be saved on disc or cassette, copied, and given to your friends, but under no circumstances may you sell them.

A cassette tape containing the programs in this book is available for the BBC Model B and the Spectrum 48K.

For the absolute beginner

Before trying to use the programs please get a knowledgeable adult or friend to teach you the following things:

How to use the keyboard
How to type in and run a program
How to save a program on cassette tape
How to load a program from cassette tape

VOLCANOES

Contents

★Pages containing computer programs,
data, or hints for using your
microcomputer are enclosed in stars★

Introducing a volcano

Volcanoes have produced some of the world's most spectacular and dangerous natural events. People have learnt to respect their power.

Some volcanoes are built up over many hundreds of years; others are built up very rapidly. From within the earth, large amounts of hot liquid rock or magma are forced upwards. Then finding a weak spot in the earth's surface it pours out of the ground as lava at the top of a volcano. As these eruptions are repeated, layer upon layer of rock is built up, so that the volcano grows larger and higher.

The drawing shows how a volcano is built up in layers over a period of time, and can threaten houses and homes in a village. ▼

◄ *After two years, the cinder cone of Parícutin had grown to a high mountain. Lava flows from the base of the cone spread over a wide area, destroying farmland and villages.*

4

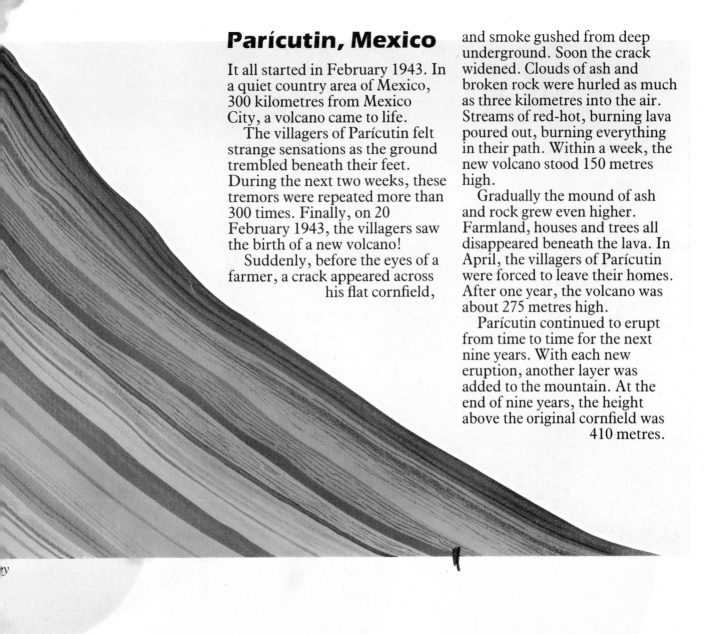

Parícutin, Mexico

It all started in February 1943. In a quiet country area of Mexico, 300 kilometres from Mexico City, a volcano came to life.

The villagers of Parícutin felt strange sensations as the ground trembled beneath their feet. During the next two weeks, these tremors were repeated more than 300 times. Finally, on 20 February 1943, the villagers saw the birth of a new volcano!

Suddenly, before the eyes of a farmer, a crack appeared across his flat cornfield, and smoke gushed from deep underground. Soon the crack widened. Clouds of ash and broken rock were hurled as much as three kilometres into the air. Streams of red-hot, burning lava poured out, burning everything in their path. Within a week, the new volcano stood 150 metres high.

Gradually the mound of ash and rock grew even higher. Farmland, houses and trees all disappeared beneath the lava. In April, the villagers of Parícutin were forced to leave their homes. After one year, the volcano was about 275 metres high.

Parícutin continued to erupt from time to time for the next nine years. With each new eruption, another layer was added to the mountain. At the end of nine years, the height above the original cornfield was 410 metres.

6 months

18 months

2 years

The church at Parícutin was nearly buried by the lava flow, and only the church spire remains above the solidified ash and cinders. ▶

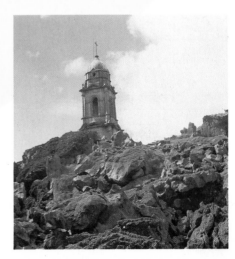

A famous eruption

Pompeii, Italy

In southern Italy, near the modern city of Naples, you can see the remains of an ancient city that was once as important as Naples itself. This was the city of Pompeii. It had remained hidden in the ground, a secret for hundreds of years, until it was discovered by chance about 200 years ago.

The Italian royal family of that time were interested in digging for ancient treasure, and their workmen would often find coins and items from the past. One day, they began to discover strange things, coated in layers of ash. Gradually the remains of shops and houses were uncovered. Later, as they dug still deeper, archaeologists were able to piece together the whole tragic story of the ancient city of Pompeii and its sudden ending nearly 2,000 years ago.

Pompeii was a large Roman city with many fine stone houses and buildings. Even public baths were built for the people – the water for these came from naturally warm underground springs. Close by the city stood an impressive cone-shaped mountain called Mount Vesuvius. It was a huge volcano, built from layers of ash and lava many years before, and people thought it was dead. Who could have realised the threat that it held?

The eruption

Suddenly, on 24 August in the year 79, the ground rumbled and an ominous black cloud appeared over the mountain top. Soon the cloud grew bigger, and the ground shook more – Vesuvius had awakened from its long sleep.

People fled in terror as the volcano erupted violently. Showers of hot ash and broken rock began to fall on the city and its people. Houses and shops quickly collapsed under the weight and heat of the ash. People and animals were buried too, as they tried to escape. Gradually Pompeii disappeared beneath deep layers of hot ash until the city was hidden.

Vesuvius became quiet and the ash stopped falling. As it slowly cooled, the ash made a thick coating over everything it touched. Gradually the dust settled, and the air cleared. Then it was possible to see that Vesuvius now had a very different shape – the whole top of the mountain was missing. The violent explosion had blown away this part of the volcano, hurling the rock onto the town below it. The hollow that was formed is called the Mount Somma crater. More recent explosions, including the last one in 1944, have helped to build up a new small cone inside this crater.

Earthquakes

A few years ago, another disaster hit Pompeii. This time it was an earthquake. Many of the Roman buildings fell because of the tremors. The ruins were closed to visitors for over a year. Now they have been restored again, and the museum is once again open to visitors. It is an exciting place to visit, if you ever get the chance.

Herculaneum

Before the eruption

After the eruption

Mount Vesuvius today

◄ *The shape of Mount Vesuvius before and after the eruption in A.D. 79, and the shape of the cone today.*

The excavated ruins of Pompeii can be seen through Caligula's Arch. Mount Vesuvius is framed in the background. ►

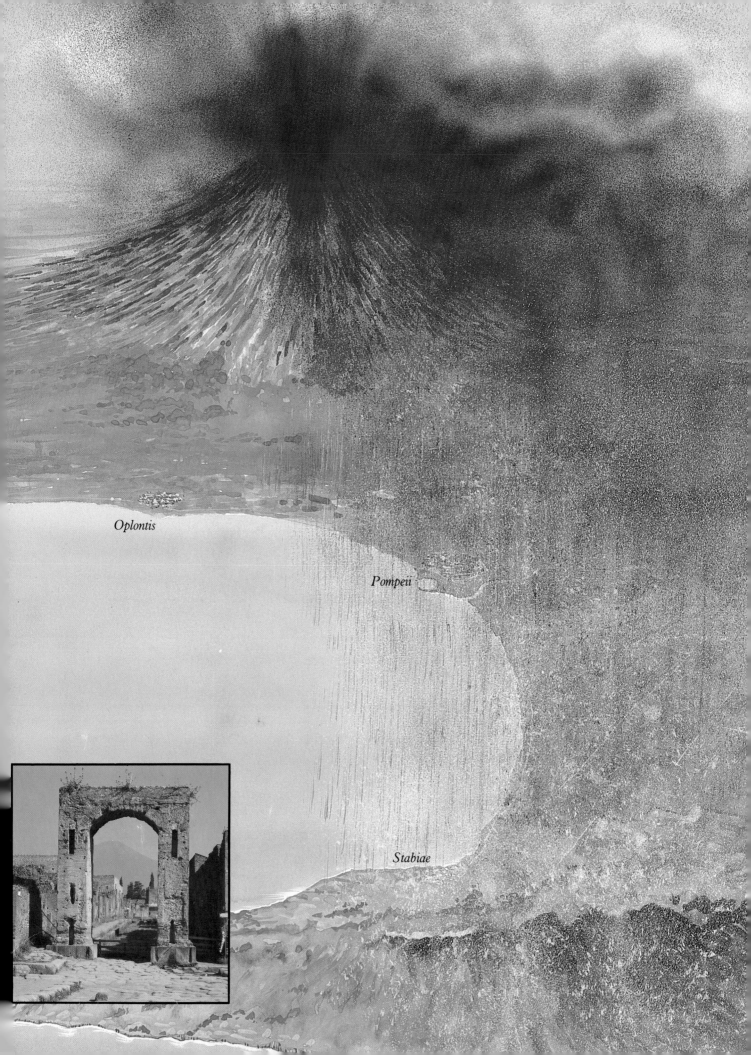

Oplontis

Pompeii

Stabiae

A famous disaster

▲ *This picture of St Pierre, looking south after the eruption, shows the total devastation of the city.*

Today St Pierre is a quiet fishing village on the shores of the bay. Mount Pelée can be seen in the background. ▼

Mount Pelée, Martinique

One of a group of beautiful volcanic islands called the Caribbean is the small island of Martinique, where you can find another volcano called Mount Pelée. Near to Mount Pelée was the busy seaport of St Pierre. It was famous for trading in sugar, rum and bananas.

The people of Martinique knew that Mount Pelée was a volcano. Sometimes it gave off a little steam, but no-one worried very much about it. But in April, 1902, the mountain made more steam than usual. Gas and ash started to reach the town too. Animals were killed by the gas, but no-one left the city.

The eruption

In early May, the volcano stirred more, and people became worried. Flows of boiling mud and ash from the volcano came close to the town, killing several

people. Still no-one left. The people didn't know it, but a large plug of rock had blocked the mouth or vent of the volcano. The hot magma was building up a terrible pressure on the plug, like a cork in a bottle.

On 8 May, disaster struck as the volcano erupted. It was 7.50 a.m. when a loud explosion rocked St Pierre. Seconds later, a burning cloud of gas and ash rushed the short distance from Mount Pelée to the town. It travelled at more than 160 kph, like a sheet of flame. People ran screaming through the streets as the glowing cloud scorched everything in its path. Many died instantly from the poisonous gas, others from terrible burns. Ships in the bay capsized in the boiling seething water. The city was devastated.

Of the 30,000 people of St Pierre, only two survived. One was a prisoner, Auguste Ciparis, saved from death by his prison cell in the dungeons. He told his story to the newspapers, and was later set free.

▲ Looking north, we can see Mount Pelée and the volcanic spine, which grew after the eruption in 1902.

The shape of Mount Pelée before, during and after the eruption in 1902. ▶

Mount Pelée today

Today, all is peaceful. The lava and ash of the volcano has weathered to make fertile soil, and forests grow right up to the crater. St Pierre is no longer the capital; it is a quiet fishing village. Only a few ruins remind visitors of its former importance – the Town Hall has gone, for instance, but its fine steps are still there. So is the prison cell.

Now that you have read about three volcanoes, you can see that they don't always erupt in the same way. People can live near volcanoes quite happily – but you can see why it is also important to understand the warning signs!

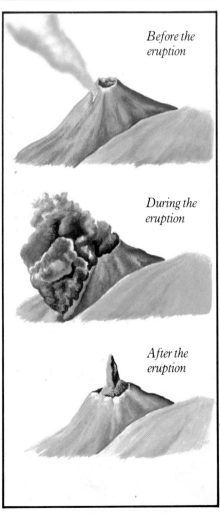

Before the eruption

During the eruption

After the eruption

How a volcano works

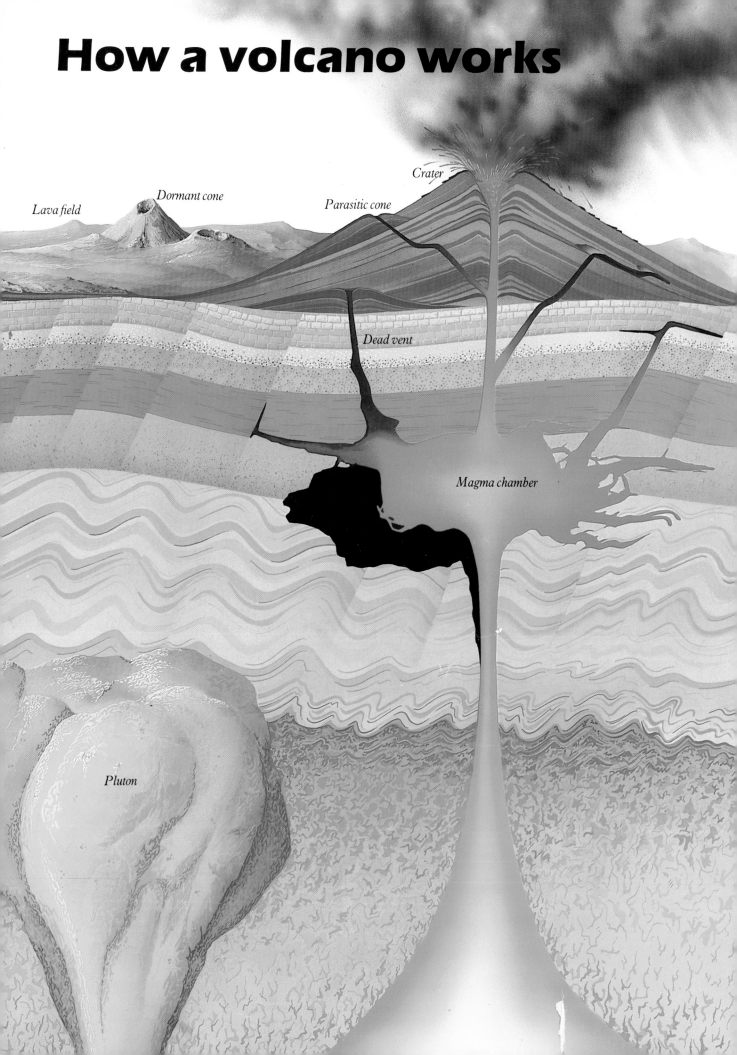

Lava field

Dormant cone

Crater

Parasitic cone

Dead vent

Magma chamber

Pluton

The lava, cinders and ash from the eruption on Heimaey in Iceland in 1973 which destroyed many houses.

A volcanic eruption is a dramatic sight, with red-hot lava flowing in streams down the mountain side, and clouds of ash and dust being spread far and wide. ▶

Volcanoes are all very different. Sometimes they are newly formed, like Parícutin. At other times, 'dead' volcanoes come to life again – much to everyone's surprise! Some volcanoes give off clouds of ash and gas, whilst others erupt in spectacular streams of dazzling, red-hot lava. To find out about these differences, we need to know more about how a volcano works.

The cone

The cone of the volcano is the part that we see on the earth's surface. Most volcanic cones are built up from layers of ash and lava, one upon the other. But this is only part of the story of a volcano. To understand how it works we must look deep underground.

Magma

Deep below the earth's surface lies molten rock, or magma.

Sometimes the magma forces its way upwards, until it lies just below the earth's crust. The liquid rocks may reach no further; they begin to cool. Crystals form, and then solid rock. If the crystals are very large, they can also be very beautiful. Rocks that are made from magma which has cooled are called igneous rocks.

Weak spots in the earth's crust allow magma to rise towards the surface. It can also 'eat' its way upwards by melting and cracking other rocks in its path. When the magma spills out of the ground, it is called lava.

As the magma rises, gases separate out from the magma. This may create extreme pressure just before the eruption, making it even more dramatic and dangerous. People living near volcanic eruptions may be killed by the burning hot gases, as were the people of St Pierre, who died from the hot blast of gas and ash from Mount Pelée.

Lava and ash

As the lava is thrown out of the volcano, the gas may make it froth and bubble. These bubbles may break up the lava into a fine spray of small droplets, which cool and set very quickly into tiny pieces of rock. Fragments of blown-up cone and rock are often thrown out with the droplets of lava, and this all falls together as ash. Larger lumps of cooled lava are called 'bombs'.

As the ash cools it sometimes welds together in the high temperatures, making solid rock. Or the hot ash may fall and cover everything, just as Vesuvius buried Pompeii.

Sometimes, bubbles are trapped inside the pieces of rock as they cool, and pockets of gas are left inside. Pumice is a volcanic rock full of bubbles – that is why it floats.

To discover why volcanoes vary so much in shape, we must find out more about lava.

This program shows a volcanic eruption. It is a simulation of how a volcano is built up layer by layer. You can choose the number of layers you want. Lava flows up from the magma chamber and out of the cone. Smoke comes from the top of the cone.

Type the program into your computer, and debug it so that it runs properly. Save the program on cassette.

```
  10 MODEl
  20 PROCSETUP
  30 REPEAT
  40    INPUT TAB(0,2),SPC(50),TAB(
0,2),"How many layers of lava do yo
u want in  your volcano",NL
  50    IF NL>9 OR NL<1 THEN OK=FAL
SE:VDU7:PRINT"Number between 1 and
9 please!" ELSE OK=TRUE
  60    UNTIL OK
  70 PRINTTAB(0,2);SPC(120);TAB(0,
0)
  80 PROCSTART
  90 FOR L%=0 TO NL-1
 100    H%=(L%+1)*YST
 110    GCOL0,1:MOVE-10,H%:MOVE-10,
H%-YST*2
 120    PLOT85,10,H%-YST*2:PLOT85,1
0,H%
 130    PROCFLOW(1)
 140    PROCPLUME
 150    PROCFLOW((L% MOD 2)+2)
 160    PS=S:S=S*0.9
 170    NEXT
 180 PRINT:PRINTTAB(0,2);"(Press a
ny key for another volcano)":Z%=GET
 190 GOTO20
 200 END


 210 DEFPROCSETUP
 220 L%=0:XST=20:YST=50:S=0.6:PS=S
 230 YOR=300:XOR=590:SP=0.2:B%=-25
0
 240 VDU29,XOR;YOR;
 250 VDU16,30,19,2,4;0;
 260 GCOL0,3:MOVE-XOR,0:PLOT1,1280
,0
 270 PROCMAGMA
 280 VDU23,230,0,0,0,7,8,16,33,32
```

```
 290 VDU23,231,0,3,156,98,65,128,
,0
 300 VDU23,232,0,0,206,49,17,136,
,2
 310 VDU23,233,64,4,4,36,34,32,25
6
 320 VDU23,234,0,0,40,40,20,19,13
,120
 330 VDU23,235,34,34,20,1,129,1,1
0,252
 340 VDU23,240,24,60,127,127,254,
54,60,24
 350 VDU23,241,&4830;&3048;&200;&
07;
 360 CLOUD$=""
 370 FOR I%=230 TO 232 : CLOUD$=C
OUD$+CHR$(I%): NEXT
 380 CLOUD$=CLOUD$+CHR$(10)+CHR$(
)+CHR$(8)+CHR$(8)
 390 FOR I%=233 TO 235 : CLOUD$=C
OUD$+CHR$(I%): NEXT
 400 ENDPROC


 410 DEFPROCMAGMA
 420 DATA-170,-200,-110,-180,-150
-260,-60,-140
 430 DATA-70,-260,70,-140,-30,-29
,110,-180
 440 DATA70,-260,170,-185,170,-29
,210,-260
 450 RESTORE 420
 460 READX%,Y%:MOVEX%,Y%:READX%,Y
:MOVEX%,Y%
 470 GCOL0,1
 480 FORI%=1TO10:READX%,Y%:PLOT85
X%,Y%
 490    NEXT
 500 ENDPROC


 510 DEFPROCSTART
 520 PRINTTAB(0,2);"Magma slowly r
oves towards the surface  from its
underground chamber"
 530 GCOL0,1:Y%=-140
 540 REPEAT MOVE-10-RND(8),Y%:DRAW
10+RND(8),Y%:Y%=Y%+4:PROCPAUSE(0.2
 550    UNTIL Y%>0
 560 PRINTTAB(0,2),"And then the e
ruption begins!";SPC(80);TAB(0,0);
 570 Y%=32
 580 MOVE-32,32:VDU5:GCOL0,3
 590 FOR I%=1 TO 50
```

```
600    J%=230+(I% MOD 5):VDU J%,J%        970    MOVEX%,Y%:PRINT CLOUD$
1                                         980    NEXT
610    Y%=Y%+RND(20):X%=RND(Y%*0.7        990 VDU4
)-Y%*0.38                                1000 ENDPROC
620    MOVEX%,Y%:PROCPAUSE(0.1)          1010 DEFPROCPAUSE(P)
630    NEXT                             1020 Z%=TIME+P*100
640 VDU4                                1030 REPEAT :UNTIL TIME>Z%
650 ENDPROC                             1040 ENDPROC
```

```
660 DEFPROCFLOW(COL)
670 GCOL0,1
680 Y2=H%:X2=10:Y1=Y2-YST:X1=10:X
=X1+XST:Y%=Y1-PS*XST
690 MOVEX1,Y1:MOVEX2,Y2:PLOT85,X%
Y%
700 MOVE-X1,Y1:MOVE-X2,Y2:PLOT85,
X%,Y%
710 X1=X2:Y1=Y2:X2=X%:Y2=Y%
720 N%=2*H%/(XST*S)
730 FOR I%=1 TO N%
740    IF(I% MOD 2)=1THENX%=X2-XST
2:Y%=Y1-S*XST ELSE X%=X1+XST:Y%=Y1
PS*XST
750    PROCBUBBLE
760    GCOL0,COL
770    IFY%<0THEN Y%=0
780    MOVEX1,Y1:MOVEX2,Y2:PLOT85,
%,Y%
790    MOVE-X1,Y1:MOVE-X2,Y2:PLOT8
,-X%,Y%
800    X1=X2:Y1=Y2:X2=X%:Y2=Y%
810    PROCPAUSE(SP)
820    NEXT
830 ENDPROC
```

```
840 DEFPROCBUBBLE
850 GCOL3,1:VDU5
860 MOVE-16,B%:VDU241
870 B%=B%+60:IF B%>H% THEN B%=-25

880 MOVE-16,B%:VDU241
890 VDU4
900 ENDPROC
```

```
910 DEFPROCPLUME
920 GCOL0,3:X%=-RND(200):Y%=H%+16
)
930 IF L%<4 THENY%=Y%+110
940 VDU5
950 FOR I%=1 TO 9
960    X%=X%+RND(80)+20:Y%=Y%+RND(
50)
```

Adding sound to the volcano

You can add sound effects to your volcano by adding the following lines. Remember that the line numbers refer to the listing as it is in the book.

```
565 SOUND0,-4,4,-1
752 ENVELOPE1,2,0,0,0,10,10,10,2,
5,-5,-1,50,126
754 IFRND(3)=2 THEN SOUND&10,1,5,
RND(15)
756 SOUND0,1,4,RND(20)
```

About the procedures

PROCSETUP *This procedure defines all the variables used later in the program, such as the speed and thickness of the lava. The VDU 23 instructions define the smoke cloud and the bubble in the lava.*

PROCMAGMA *This draws in the magma chamber. The shape of the chamber is stored in the DATA statements as x and y coordinates. The chamber is filled in by using the PLOT85 instruction (line 480). If you want to see how the shape is filled in add the line*
485 PROCPAUSE(1)
but remember to delete it from the program afterwards.

PROCSTART *This draws the lava rising from the magma chamber to the surface. A rising cloud of steam and ash is sketched in.*

PROCFLOW *This is the most important part of the program. It uses animation to show the red hot lava flowing down the sides of the volcano. As the lava flows a bubble of gas rises up the lava tube.*

PROCPLUME *This procedure adds more clouds to the ash cloud above the volcano.*

PROCPAUSE(P) *This is a useful procedure which keeps the computer busy doing nothing, so that you can put pauses into the program. For example, PROCPAUSE(3) makes the computer wait for 3 seconds before carrying on.*

Shapes

Flat shape

Volcanoes have many shapes and sizes. Some may be steep and pointed like Fujiyama in Japan. Others are so flat that at first sight they do not look cone-shaped at all. These different shapes are made by different types of lava and different types of eruption.

Lava is made of several different chemical ingredients. Because of this, some lava is thin and runny, so it flows quite easily. This is called non-viscous lava and it sometimes runs in streams for several kilometres, making a large but flat volcano like Mauna Loa, whose name means 'long mountain'.

Streams of non-viscous lava flow down the shallow sides of Kilauea in Hawaii, the world's largest active volcano.

Steep shape

At the other extreme, lava can be much more thick and sticky like treacle. This is called viscous lava. It does not flow very easily, and it sets quickly round the vent. Sometimes this thick viscous lava squeezes out of the vent and sets as a sharp point called a spine. However, most volcanoes come between these two extremes.

As soon as the lava is thrown out of the volcano, it begins to cool. The air helps to lower the temperature of the lava and as it gets cooler, it begins to set. The rate at which lava cools varies a great deal. Thick streams of lava cool more slowly; some may not cool for several months.

The surface of the lava cools and

El Teide on Tenerife in the Canary Islands is an example of a steep-sided volcano formed by sticky viscous lava.

A solidified lava flow in Tenerife showing the kind of blocky shapes typical of viscous lava. ▶

Cross-section of the cone of a volcano formed by layers of non-viscous lava. ▼

The consistency of lava is one of the main things that affects the shape of a volcano. Runny lava produces a flat shape, and sticky lava a steep-sided shape. Most volcanoes are between these two extremes.

▲ *Cross-section of the cone of a steep-sided volcano formed by layers of viscous lava.*

sets first, like the skin on custard. People can sometimes walk on this 'skin', whilst below their feet, the lava may still be red hot.

If the lava flows under water or ice the cooling is more rapid. The surface may set into strange shapes and make the volcano sides even steeper. This may still happen even if the lava is the runny or non-viscous type, because of the fast cooling.

The type of lava therefore helps control the shape of the volcano. The thicker or more viscous the lava is, and the more quickly it sets, the steeper the shape will be.

More shapes

Magma pushes up through the sea floor to make a new underwater volcano.

As the volcano erupts, the lava flow forms a new island.

The lava cools quickly under the sea, and the island grows rapidly.

We usually think of volcanoes as a perfect cone shape, but this is not always true. The outline of the cone can be changed by other minor eruptions, and by erosion over the years.

Occasionally the vent of a volcano gets blocked with a plug of hard lava. This causes pressure to build up below ground, until something must give way. Sometimes, instead of the main vent blowing, the magma will find a new route to the surface. It may emerge at the side of the main volcano as a parasitic cone. An example of this is Vulcanello, a mini-cone that appeared at the side of Vulcano in the Lipari Islands.

In some volcanoes the pressure builds up, like a bottle of fizzy drink when it is shaken, until there is a violent explosion. This can blow off the top of the mountain in seconds, leaving a huge hollow or crater called a caldera. Later the crater sometimes gets filled with rainwater, making a big lake.

Such dramatic explosions have happened to many volcanoes. Vesuvius exploded burying Pompeii under ash and rock. In 1980 Mount St Helens in America blew out the side of the volcano, scattering more than a cubic kilometre of ash over a very large area. As a result, the height of St Helens was reduced by some 400 metres.

Many volcanoes have changed shape over the years because their sides have been worn away by rivers, ice, or even rain. This is called erosion. Volcanoes made of ash are worn away more quickly than those made of solid lava. Heavy rain may turn the ash into sticky mud-flows, which

◄ *In 1973 an underwater eruption in the Atlantic Ocean formed the new island of Surtsey within two days. The diagrams show how the island was built up from the sea floor as the lava flow increased.*

n be very dangerous. Deep
lleys can be left where the side
the mountain has been washed
ay. The mud helps to make
rtile soils nearby, which are
ry useful for agriculture.
Sometimes the volcanic plug is
that remains of a volcano. It
n make a spectacular feature in
e landscape. Edinburgh Castle
Scotland overlooks Edinburgh
om a site on top of an ancient
lcanic plug. If you go to the
uvergne region of the Massif
entral in France, you will see
all rocky hills that rise
ddenly out of the land. These
e also hard volcanic plugs, all
at are left after the sides of the
iginal volcanoes have been
orn away. The most famous of
ese plugs is the one in the town
Le Puy, which, although it is
all, somehow has a church
rched on top of it.

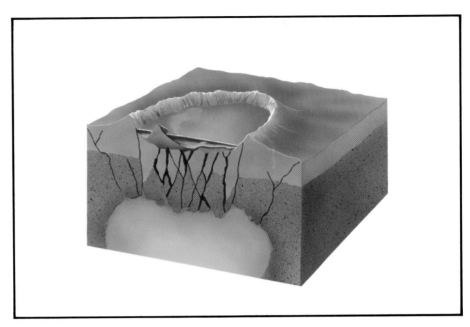

▲ *When the top of a volcano is blown off, a crater or caldera is formed. This may fill with water to form a lake. Often a new cone develops in the floor of the caldera as further eruptions occur.*

A crater lake was formed in northern Japan after the explosion of an ancient volcano which people call Mount Zao-San. The lake is a green colour in the sunlight. ▼

Volcano models

Make your own Vesuvius

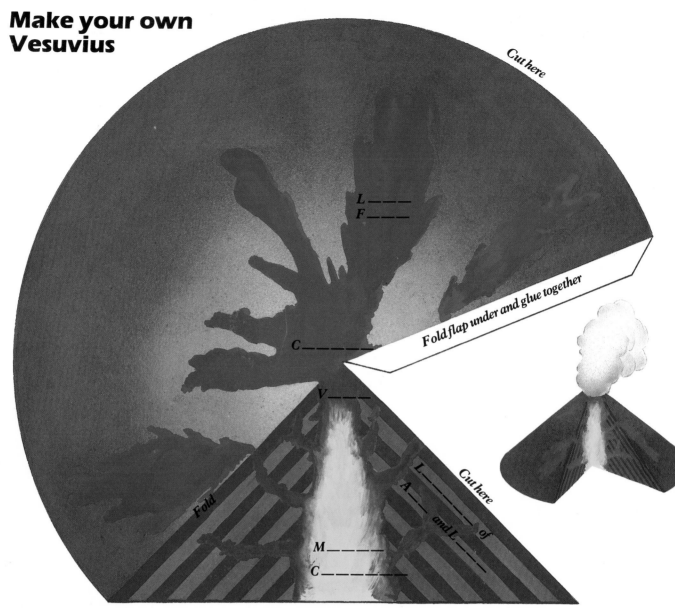

Cut here

L _ _ _
F _ _ _

Fold flap under and glue together

C _ _ _ _ _ _

V _ _ _ _

Fold

Cut here

L _ _ _ _ _ _ _ _ *of*
A _ _ _ *and L*

M _ _ _ _ _ _
C _ _ _ _ _ _ _

1 Trace the outline of the model on to paper.

2 Label the volcano using the beginning letters of the words to help you as follows:

Vent   Crater   Lava flows

Magma chamber   Layers of ash and lava

3 Colour the volcano to show the hot lava flows; the dusty layers of ash and fragments; the rocky and grassy surface of the volcano.

4 Cut out the model along the solid lines.

5 Fold along the dotted lines.

6 Glue the flap and stick your model togethe

7 Find some cotton wool to colour and stick at the top for smoke.

Try this working volcano

You must only attempt this under adult supervision.

1 Make a volcano shape in sand on a large tray, and hollow out a small crater at the top.

2 Take the sand model out of doors and put it in a safe place. (Note – this model must not be done indoors.)

3 Ask your science teacher or an adult to plac a small amount of ammonium dichromate in the crater and to light it carefully.

*4 **Stand well back.** Do not approach the crater, even if nothing seems to be happening Just as with real volcanoes, an eruption can be unexpected!*

5 Hey presto! Ash will come out of the cone and land in layers on the side of the volcano. It will keep making more and more and more ash!

A simple but safe volcano

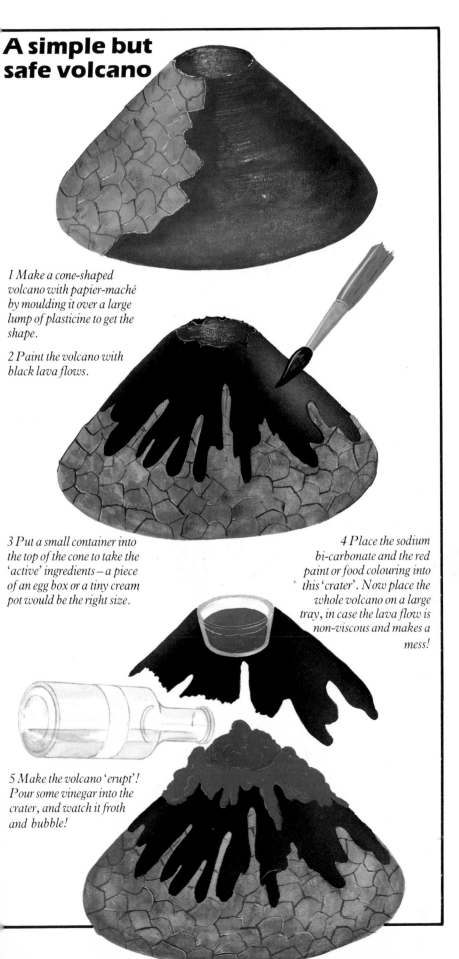

1 Make a cone-shaped volcano with papier-maché by moulding it over a large lump of plasticine to get the shape.

2 Paint the volcano with black lava flows.

3 Put a small container into the top of the cone to take the 'active' ingredients – a piece of an egg box or a tiny cream pot would be the right size.

4 Place the sodium bi-carbonate and the red paint or food colouring into this 'crater'. Now place the whole volcano on a large tray, in case the lava flow is non-viscous and makes a mess!

5 Make the volcano 'erupt'! Pour some vinegar into the crater, and watch it froth and bubble!

More ideas for making volcanoes

1 Try making a volcano cake. You will need either a pudding basin shape to make a cone, or you will have to use a very sticky cake-mixture, so that it stands up in a cone shape. Another way would be to use layers of different coloured sponge, with cream icing in between them.

2 An easy way to make good lava flows is to use Ice-Magic, the ice-cream topping. The 'lava' sets very quickly, and the next 'eruption' of lava should do one of three things. Either, it gets blocked by the first flow. Or, it pushes the first flow in front of it. Or, it flows right over the top of it. Of course, it is also good to eat!

3 If you have a kit for making candles, you can buy or make a cone-shaped mould, and then you will be able to make lots of burning volcanoes. They will probably have craters and lava flows as well!

19

Other volcanic features

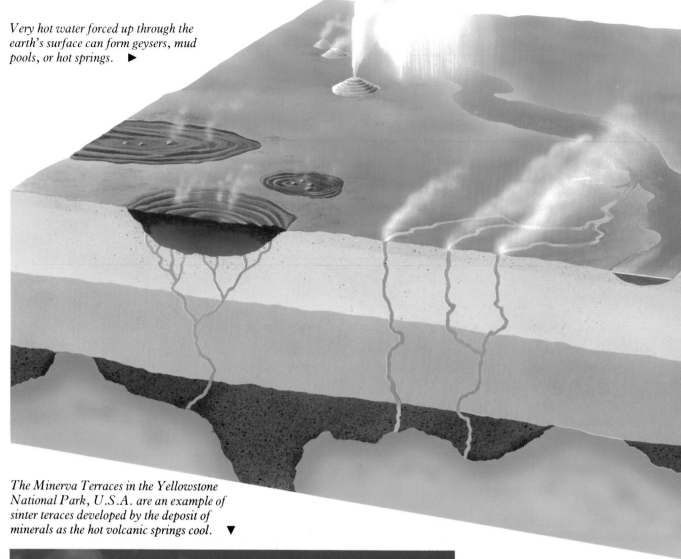

Very hot water forced up through the earth's surface can form geysers, mud pools, or hot springs. ▶

The Minerva Terraces in the Yellowstone National Park, U.S.A. are an example of sinter teraces developed by the deposit of minerals as the hot volcanic springs cool. ▼

Apart from erupting volcanoes and lava flows, there are other natural features which show that an area is volcanic. Near some recently active volcanoes, cracks or holes in the ground called fumaroles are often found. Steam and volcanic gases escape from these fumaroles, and the surrounding rocks are much hotter than usual.

Hot springs are often found near volcanoes, although not all hot springs are in volcanic areas. Rainwater sinks into the ground and is heated by the hot volcanic rocks. These rocks contain many mineral salts which dissolve in

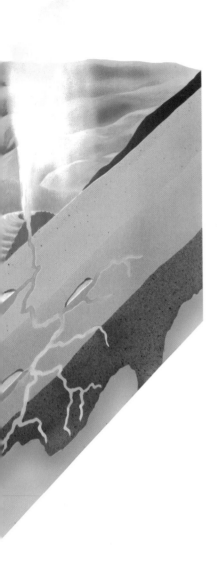

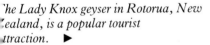
The Lady Knox geyser in Rotorua, New Zealand, is a popular tourist attraction. ▶

he hot water. Where the heated water emerges as a hot spring, people often bathe, or drink the water of the spring, because they believe the minerals in the water are good for their health.

Some hot springs have beautiful coloured rock formations known as sinter terraces. These rocks form slowly over a long period of time from the minerals carried by the hot water. When the water cools, the minerals are deposited as solid material, which builds up over the years into fantastic shapes. These mineral deposits are known as evaporite deposits.

A hot spring which spurts out hot water and steam is called a geyser. The rocks below the geyser act rather like a giant pressure cooker. Super-heated water below the ground gets so hot that it starts to boil and push water out to the surface. This makes the pressure drop suddenly, and the mass of water suddenly boils, and is ejected into the air in a brief spurt of steam and water. The geyser becomes quiet, and the water seeps back underground for the whole heating up process to start again. The largest and most spectacular geysers are found in

the Yellowstone National Park in the United States, in particular Old Faithful, which is famous for ejecting water regularly at hourly intervals for more than a hundred years.

Sometimes a mud pool forms instead of a hot spring. Hot water and gases from beneath the surface bubble through the mud. The result looks and sounds like a pan of simmering porridge! Sulphurous gases give the mud an evil smell, but the minerals in the mud are often thought to have healing properties, so the mud pools may be health centres as well as tourist attractions.

This program is an expanded version of Build with further animated effects. You choose whether the lava is sticky or runny. Rock and ash are flung into the air. Sometimes there is a further eruption which forms a caldera. You can add sound effects which make the volcano hiss and sizzle.

This program shows only sticky or runny lava. Real volcanoes usually behave somewhere between these two extremes.

Here is what you must do.

1. Load Build into your computer from cassette.

2. Type in a new control routine as follows:

```
10 MODE1
20 DIM XP(16),YP(16),VV(8),VH(8)
30 PROCSETUP
40 PROCLTYPE
50 REPEAT
60    PROCERUPT
70    UNTIL H%>110
80 PROCPAUSE(2)
90 IF L$="R" THEN PROCNOCALD ELS
E PROCCALD
100 *FX15,1
110 PRINT:COLOUR1:PRINT"(Press an
y key for another volcano)":Z%=GET:
COLOUR3
120 GOTO30
130 END
```

3. Type in DELETE 140,200 to remove the rest of the control routine for Build.

4. Type in the following after the procedures for Build.

```
1500 DEFPROCLTYPE
1510 PRINTTAB(0,3);"Choose the typ
e of lava for the volcano"
1520 REPEAT
1530    INPUT "Runny (R) or Sticky
(S)",L$
1540    L$=LEFT$(L$,1)
1550    UNTIL L$="R" OR L$="S"
1560 IFL$="R"THEN S=0.3:SP=0.05:EJ
=0:YST=20 ELSE S=0.6:SP=0.2:EJ=1:YS
T=40
1570 PS=S:PRINTTAB(0,3);SPC(120)
1580 ENDPROC
```

```
1590 DEFPROCERUPT
1600 REPEAT
1610    OK=TRUE
1620    INPUTTAB(0,2),SPC(35),TAB(
,2),"How many layers of lava",NL
1630    IF NL+L%>9 OR NL<1 THEN OK
FALSE:VDU7:PRINT "Between 1 and ";
-L%;" please!";TAB(0,2),SPC(30)
1640    UNTIL OK
1650 PRINTTAB(0,2);SPC(80);TAB(0,
)
1660 IF L%=0 THEN PROCSTART
1670 FOR C%=0 TO NL-1
1680    H%=(L%+1)*YST
1690    PROCEXPL(EJ)
1700    GCOL0,1:MOVE-10,H%:MOVE-10
H%-YST*2
1710    PLOT85,10,H%-YST*2:PLOT85,
0,H%
1720    PROCFLOW(1):PROCPLUME
1730    PROCFLOW((L% MOD 2)+2)
1740    PS=S:S=S*0.9:L%=L%+1
1750    NEXT
1760 ENDPROC
```

```
1770 DEFPROCEXPL(FL)
1780 T=0:TSTEP=2:YLLIM=0:G=-5
1790 IF FL=1 THEN YLLIM=YLLIM+32
1800 VDU5:GCOL3,1
1810 FORI%=1TO8
1820    XP(I%)=RND(100)-50:YP(I%)=
%-RND(100)
1830    VH(I%)=RND(30)+10
1840    IFRND(2)=2THENVH(I%)=-VH(I
)
1850    VV(I%)=40+RND(50)
1860    NEXT
1870 REPEAT
1880    PROCDRAW
1890    T=T+TSTEP:FIN=TRUE
1900    FORI%=9TO16
1910       YP(I%)=(G*T+VV(I%-8))*T+
%
1920       IFYP(I%)>YLLIM THEN FIN=F
ALSE:XP(I%)=VH(I%-8)*T ELSE YP(I%)=
YLLIM
1930       NEXT
1940    PROCDRAW
1950    FORI%=1TO8
1960       XP(I%)=XP(I%+8):YP(I%)=YP
(I%+8)
1970       NEXT
1980    UNTIL FIN
1990 GCOL0,3:PROCDRAW:VDU4
2000 ENDPROC
```

```
2010 DEFPROCDRAW                           2400    MOVEXC,YC:PLOT85,XC-R*CT,YC
2020 FOR J%=1 TO 8                         -R*ST
2030    MOVEXP(J%),YP(J%)                  2410    NEXT
2040    IF FL=1 THEN VDU240 ELSE PL        2420 ENDPROC
 65,0,0
2050    NEXT
2060 ENDPROC                               2430 DEFPROCCOOLV
                                           2440 GCOL0,3:Y%=H%-YST/4
                                           2450 REPEAT MOVE -10-RND(8),Y%:PLO
2070 DEFPROCNOCALD                         T1,20+RND(16),0:Y%=Y%-4:PROCPAUSE(0
2080 PROCERASM                             .2)
2090 PRINTTAB(0,0);"The volcano co         2460    UNTIL Y%<-20
 s down .."                                2470 ENDPROC
2100 PROCCOOLV
2110 PRINT"and becomes dormant."
2120 ENDPROC                               2480 DEFPROCERASM
                                           2490 GCOL0,0:Y%=1024
                                           2500 FOR I%=1TO6
2130 DEFPROCCALD                           2510    Y%=1024+4*I%
2140 PROCERASM                             2520    REPEAT
2150 PRINTTAB(0,0);"The volcano co         2530       MOVE-XOR,Y%:PLOT1,1280,0:
 s down .."                                Y%=Y%-24:PROCPAUSE(0.1)
2160 PROCPAUSE(2):PROCCOOLV                2540       UNTIL Y%<H%
2170 PRINT"and the magma pressure          2550    PROCPAUSE(1)
 ilds up below  the plug ..":PROCP         2560    NEXT
 USE(3)                                    2570 GCOL0,3
2180 PRINT"until .. ";                     2580 ENDPROC
2190 GCOL0,0:MOVE0,-20:MOVE-20,H%/
 :PLOT85,20,H%/2
2200 PROCSEMIC(0,H%,H%/2)
2210 VDU5:GCOL0,3
2220 FOR I%=1 TO 50
2230    MOVE RND(200)-110,H%/2+RND(
 *H%)
2240    VDU230+(I% MOD 6)                  Adding sound to the volcano
2250    NEXT                               You can add sound to the volcano by adding the following lines.
2260 VDU4:PRINT"an eruption makes           Remember that the line numbers refer to the listing as it is shown
 caldera"; :VDU5                           in the book and if you renumber the program the line numbers
2270 FOR P%=1 TO 6                         will not be the same.
2280    FOR I%=1 TO 5
2290       MOVE RND(200)-110,H%/2+RN          565 SOUND0,-4,4,-1
 (2*H%)                                       752 ENVELOPE1,2,0,0,0,10,10,10,2,
2300       VDU5,230+I%                     5,-5,-1,50,126
2310       NEXT I%                            754 IFRND(3)=2 THEN SOUND&10,1,5,
2320    PROCEXPL(1)                        RND(15)
2330    NEXT P%                               756 SOUND0,1,4,RND(20)
2340 ENDPROC                                 1864 ENVELOPE2,2,0,0,0,10,10,10,20
                                           ,-1,0,-1,126,100
                                             1866 SOUND&10,2,6,20:SOUND0,2,4,15
2350 DEFPROCSEMIC(XC,YC,R)
2360 N%=20:MOVEXC-R,YC
2370 CD=COS(2*PI/N%):SD=SIN(2*PI/N
 ):CT=1:ST=0                               Experimenting with circles
2380 FORI%=1TON%/2                         With a couple of changes to PROCSEMIC it is easy to write a
2390    NCT=CT*CD-ST*SD:NST=ST*CD+C        procedure which draws filled in circles. Make sure you have
 *SD:CT=NCT:ST=NST                         saved the program on cassette and then type in these lines:
                                           2350 DEFPROCCIRCLE(XC,YC,R)
                                           2380 FOR I%=1TON%
                                           To see what this does type in
                                           GCOL0,1:PROCCIRCLE(600,500,200)
                                           Try experimenting with different numbers.
```

Disasters

116th Year No. 107 ★★★ TUESDAY, MAY 20, 1980 777-1111 20 CENTS

Many Hikers Are Missing
Volcano Toll May Grow

Ash Still Boiling Into Air

Black cloud blots sun

Volcano's ash found in Colorad

By John Yammanley
and Joanne Grant
Staff Writer

Ash Chokes West

116th Year No. 106 ★★★ MONDAY, MAY 19, 1980 777-1111 20 Ce

Boiling Fury

Eruption Kills 5 — Gigantic Ash Cloud

Mt. St. Helens Spews Mud, Causes Floods

By Charles Peto

Missing-persons total nears 100

by Hill Williams
Times science reporter

More inside:

St. Helens let go with a tremendous blast yesterday

Airline Pilot's View of The Awesome Display

By Robert Bartlett

Index

Bridge	27
Business World	28
Chess	27
Comics	29
Deaths	34
Entertainment	39
People	39
TV-Radio	60
Weather	22
	58
	39

Top of the News on Page 20

Huge Forest Fires
THE VOLCANO BLOWS UP

The headlines from newspapers published at the time of the Mount St Helens eruption describe the extent of the devastation and human tragedy it caused

The eruptions of Mount St Helens in the north-west United States in 1980 were recorded in great detail by both scientists and news reporters. The main eruption and landslide was triggered by an earthquake.

Immediately, a blast of hot gases and steam flattened forests up to 27 kilometres away. The blast sent ash and rocks high into the air. Valleys were buried, people and animals were choked to death. Floods and mud flows caused more devastation. A great ash storm, with lightning, turned daylight into night 140 kilometres away from the mountain. Towns and rivers were choked with ash, and farmland was ruined.

Newspaper headlines give the dramatic story, but many human tragedies follow in the wake of a volcanic eruption. People have to abandon their homes and may never see them again. Even if the houses survive and the people can return, there may be a lot of mess to clear up. Nobody wants to live in a dangerous place, so people will be unable to sell their houses and move to a safe area.

A cloud of ash and rocks was hurled into the air when Mount St Helens erupted in 1980. ▶

Insurance companies will probably refuse to insure the homes because they are a bad risk.

Water is a big problem, and floods are highly likely. Steam from the crater will fall as heavy rain, and ash and lava can block river valleys. Lakes will form behind the debris. But water is heavy, and ash deposits are not strong. The weight of the water could break the new dam suddenly, with disastrous results.

Despite the floods, there may be a shortage of drinking water. The earthquakes that often accompany eruptions will break the water pipes and sewers. Water becomes dangerous to drink because it may be polluted – that is, if you can get any water to drink at all.

Roads and railways will be blocked by earthquakes, landslides or lava flows. All the normal supply routes may be out of action. Food will be in short supply, and disease will spread. Doctors will be busy with injured people and medicines will be hard to obtain. In Indonesia in 1815, when Tambora erupted, about 12,000 people died at once. However, 70,000 more died from the famine and the disease which followed the eruption.

If a volcano erupts in the sea, a giant wave called a tsunami could form and surge inland, destroying everything in its path. About 36,000 people were drowned in Indonesia by the tsunami which followed the great eruption of Krakatoa in 1883.

The blast of hot gases and steam following the eruption flattened the forests, and left them looking like an untidy pile of matchsticks. ▶

Benefits

Volcanoes are usually thought of as spectacular and destructive, but there can also be benefits to living in a volcanic area.

Electricity

Hot springs in Iceland provide hot water for cheap central heating, a great benefit in a country with cold winters and no coal or oil. The hot water heats the greenhouses as well, allowing vegetables to be grown near the Arctic circle. In Italy and New Zealand some electricity generators are powered by steam hissing out of the ground. Several other countries are planning to use geothermal

◄ *On the terraced vineyards of La Gomera in the Canary Islands, luscious grapes are grown in the rich volcanic soil.*

energy by pumping water below ground to be heated up by hot rocks.

Agriculture

The most widespread benefit from volcanoes is not at all spectacular, but very important. New lava is rough and lifeless, but old, weathered lava can make very good soil. Lava contains many minerals needed by plants for strong healthy growth. Good crops often come from areas with volcanic soil. The tea plantations of Kenya are on volcanic soils. Java in Indonesia can support 0 million people because the

Basalt is mined at Hofeld in the Rhineland of Germany. The hexagonal pillar structure is typical of basalt deposits. ▶

volcanic soil is so rich. Hawaii has lush vegetation. The volcanic soils of the Canary Islands produce grapes, tomatoes and potatoes. In the Mediterranean, the Italian island of Lampedusa is almost useless, dry limestone; a few miles away, volcanic Pantellaria grows superb grapes and every tiny piece of land is carefully cultivated.

Tourism

Volcanoes can be very beautiful, like Fujiyama in Japan, but old volcanic areas, long since dead, can also provide lovely countryside. Many of the world's rocks are left from previous volcanic eras, millions of years ago. In some places, glaciers and ice-sheets have eroded volcanic rocks. Such areas provide beautiful scenery, and many are now preserved as

◀ *The spectacular scenery of Grasmere in the Lake District was formed by glacial erosion of ancient volcanic rocks.*

National Parks which are visited by many people each year.

Construction

Volcanic deposits and igneous rocks have many uses. Volcanic ash can be used to make building blocks, and pumice is used as an insulator in buildings. Pumice can be ground to a fine powder and used as an abrasive. Millions of tons of igneous rocks are used every year as road chippings, and ballast for railway tracks. The more beautiful rocks, such as larvikite, are polished and used to decorate public buildings.

Mining

Around the pluton, or roots of an old volcano, can be a rich source of metals such as gold and copper. The high value of these metals makes them worth the expense of mining them. The richest source of diamonds in the world is within the ancient volcanic rocks near Kimberley in South Africa.

Volcano vacation

Between the Italian mainland and the large island of Sicily, there is a group of seven volcanic islands called the Lipari Islands. Each island is different, but together they possess most of the volcanic features discussed in this book.

You can visit the Lipari Islands by taking the overnight boat from Naples. At dawn you are close to Stromboli, the only continuously active volcano in the group. There is no harbour, so you clamber into rowing boats with the other passengers to reach the shore. Other ferries and smaller boats enable travel from one island to the next. A trip round the Lipari Islands makes an unusual and interesting vacation. It provides an opportunity for first hand experience of many volcanic features.

▲ Every fifteen minutes, the earth shakes as the volcano on Stromboli erupts. Fortunately the lava usually falls back into the crater.

Alicudi is the most remote of the seven islands. It is a perfect volcano shape, with an extinct volcano 675 metres high in the centre. Only 700 people live here; they are mostly shepherds and fishermen. Few tourists reach Alicudi.

Filicudi

Alicudi

Filicudi has 1500 people. They are mostly farmers growing crops on the fertile volcanic soil. You can visit an impressive basalt cave on the west coast.

Salina has two extinct volcanoes. One of them is the highest volcano in the seven islands – 962 metres (nearly as high as Snowdon). From the top you can see all the other islands. The volcanic soil is very fertile, and Salina's excellent grapes make good wine.

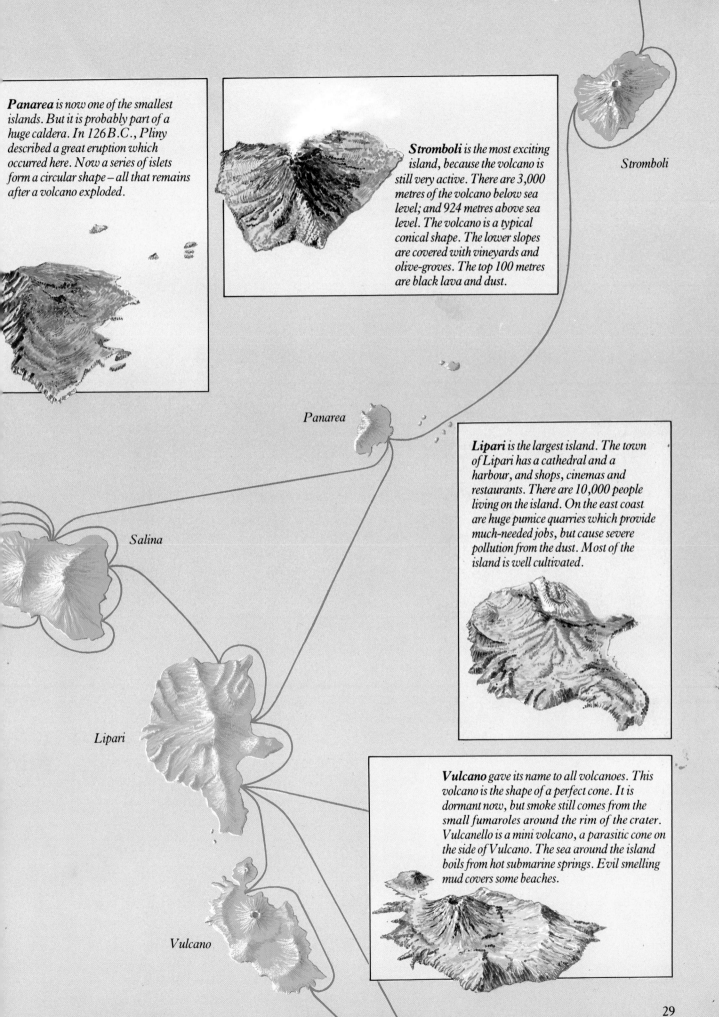

Panarea *is now one of the smallest islands. But it is probably part of a huge caldera. In 126 B.C., Pliny described a great eruption which occurred here. Now a series of islets form a circular shape – all that remains after a volcano exploded.*

Stromboli *is the most exciting island, because the volcano is still very active. There are 3,000 metres of the volcano below sea level; and 924 metres above sea level. The volcano is a typical conical shape. The lower slopes are covered with vineyards and olive-groves. The top 100 metres are black lava and dust.*

Stromboli

Panarea

Lipari *is the largest island. The town of Lipari has a cathedral and a harbour, and shops, cinemas and restaurants. There are 10,000 people living on the island. On the east coast are huge pumice quarries which provide much-needed jobs, but cause severe pollution from the dust. Most of the island is well cultivated.*

Salina

Lipari

Vulcano *gave its name to all volcanoes. This volcano is the shape of a perfect cone. It is dormant now, but smoke still comes from the small fumaroles around the rim of the crater. Vulcanello is a mini volcano, a parasitic cone on the side of Vulcano. The sea around the island boils from hot submarine springs. Evil smelling mud covers some beaches.*

Vulcano

29

The program shows you a map of the island of Disaster. There are three villages on the island: Ashville, Bubblecombe, and Corruption. These are marked A, B, and C on the map. Both the Geyser Hills and the Lava Mountains are volcanic and eruptions occur frequently. You are the Health and Safety Officer for the island. It is your job to keep track of eruptions. You have two instruments to help you: a tilt meter and a vibration meter. You can move them round the island with the cursor keys and fix their position by pressing any other key. You receive measurements daily and you must guess when and where the next eruption is likely to happen. Press ESCAPE to exit the program, and type RUN to play again.

Type the program into your computer and debug it so that it runs properly. Save the program on cassette. (Procedures in this program are used in Newsflash.)

```
 10 MODE2
 20 VDU28,0,31,19,24
 30 PROCISLAND
 40 PROCSETUP
 50 REPEAT
 60   PROCUPDATE:PROCPAUSE(1.5)
 70   UNTIL FINISH
 80 PROCFINALE
 90 END


100 DEFPROCISLAND
110 DATA140,510,210,660,240,370,245,840
120 DATA320,320,260,940,490,315,330,970
130 DATA600,305,410,960,705,330,510,940
140 DATA790,335,670,1000,900,365,740,950
150 DATA1040,310,810,960,1130,330,965,750
160 DATA1190,380,1000,710,1180,500,1065,680,1260
,660,1130,700,-1
170 DATA1135,960,990,930,950,1000,965,860

180 DATA810,960,965,750,1130,330,-2
190 GCOL0,4:PROCRECT(0,256,1280,800)
200 GCOL0,0:PROCFILL
210 PROCFOREST:PROCRIVER
220 PROCMOUNTS:PROCROAD:PROCVILLAGES
230 ENDPROC


240 DEFPROCFOREST
250 DATA1010,380,1140,420,950,400,1070,350,840,4
20,760,365,-1
260 REPEAT
270   READX%:IFX%>0THEN READ Y%:MOVEX%,Y%:PROCTR
EE(2+RND(1)*2)
280   UNTILX%<0
290 ENDPROC


300 DEFPROCTREE(S)
310 GCOL0,2:PLOT1,0,32*S
320 FORI%=1TO2
330   PLOT0,-8*S,-8*S:PLOT1,8*S,8*S
340   PLOT1,8*S,-8*S:PLOT0,-8*S,-4*S
350   NEXT
360 ENDPROC
```

```
370 DEFPROCRIVER
380 DATA165,570,185,612,204,516,204,516,310,46
390 DATA500,520,520,580,500,620,540,650,596,63
400 DATA730,590,776,592,808,628,832,664,872,68
940,650,-1
410 GCOL0,4:READX%,Y%:MOVEX%,Y%
420 READX%,Y%:MOVEX%,Y%:READX%,Y%:PLOT85,X%,Y%
430 GCOL0,6:PROCLINE
440 ENDPROC


450 DEFPROCMOUNTS
460 DATA4,796,568,880,604,916,580,876,556,936,
0,988,548
470 DATA956,584,1008,668,1064,588,960,536,1096
04,1168,560
480 DATA6,244,772,308,812,456,764,384,792,420,
0,452,792
490 DATA436,776,496,828,528,804,436,752,544,81
624,748
500 DATA564,796,608,840,660,792,356,804,476,89
584,820
510 GCOL0,7
520 FORK%=1TO2
530   READN%
540   FOR I%=1TON%
550     READX%,Y%:MOVEX%,Y%
560     FORJ%=1TO2:READX%,Y%:DRAWX%,Y%:NEXT
570   NEXT I%:NEXT K%
580 ENDPROC


590 DEFPROCROAD
600 DATA348,348,444,368,532,344,608,420,596,50
628,568
610 DATA656,664,748,712,768,812,848,836,892,88
948,904,-2
620 GCOL0,3:PROCLINE
630 ENDPROC


640 DEFPROCVILLAGES
650 PROCPLOSTR(256,440,7,"A")
660 PROCPLOSTR(880,936,7,"B")
670 PROCPLOSTR(1132,672,7,"C")
680 GCOL0,0:PROCRECT(980,900,64,16)
690 GCOL0,7:PROCCHURCH
700 ENDPROC


710 DEFPROCCHURCH
720 PROCRECT(328,372,40,40)
730 PLOT0,-20,0:PLOT1,0,40:PLOT0,-20,-14
740 PLOT1,40,0
750 ENDPROC


760 DEFPROCRECT(X,Y,L,H)
770 MOVEX,Y:PLOT0,0,H
780 PLOT81,L,-H:PLOT81,0,H
790 ENDPROC


800 DEFPROCPLOSTR(X,Y,C,S$)
810 VDU5:GCOL0,C:MOVEX,Y:PRINT S$
820 VDU4:GCOL0,7
830 ENDPROC


840 DEFPROCLINE
850 READ X%,Y%:MOVEX%,Y%
860 READ X%:IF X%>=0 THEN READ Y%:DRAWX%,Y% EI
ENDPROC
870 GOTO 860


880 DEFPROCFILL
890 REPEAT
900   READX%,Y%:MOVEX%,Y%:READX%,Y%:MOVEX%,Y%
910   REPEAT
920     READ X%:IFX%>-1THEN READ Y%:PLOT85,X%
930     UNTIL X%<0
940   UNTIL X%<-1
950 ENDPROC
```

```
 960 DEFPROCSETUP
 970 PROCSETERUPTION
 980 PROCPUTMETERS
 990 PROCHEADER
1000 W%=1:D%=1:FINISH=FALSE:G$="N"
1010 ENDPROC
1020 DEFPROCSETERUPTION
1030 EWK=RND(4)+2:EDAY=RND(7)
1040 IF RND(3)=2 THEN EX=800:EY=500 ELSEEX=350:EY
50
1050 EX=EX+RND(300):EY=EY+RND(150)
1060 ENDPROC


1070 DEFPROCPUTMETERS
1080 COLOUR3
1090 PRINTTAB(0,1);"Move the detectors  with the
rsor keysFix with any other  key"
1100 COLOUR7
1110 FOR I%=1 TO 2
1120   IF I%=1 THEN CUR$="T" ELSE CUR$="V"
1130   REPEAT
1140     PROCCURSOR(CUR$)
1150     IF POINT(X%,Y%)=4 THEN INSEA=TRUE:VDU7:P
CPLOSTR(X%,Y%,4,CUR$) ELSE INSEA=FALSE
1160     UNTIL NOT INSEA
1170   X%=X%+16:Y%=Y%-16
1180   D%=SQR((EX-X%)^2+(EY-Y%)^2)/2
1190   IF I%=1 THEN TDIST=D% ELSE VDIST=D%
1200   NEXT I%
1210 ENDPROC


1220 DEFPROCCURSOR(CUR$)
1230 *FX4,1
1240 *FX15,1
1250 VDU5:GCOL3,5:X%=640:Y%=560
1260 MOVEX%,Y%:PRINT CUR$
1270 REPEAT
1280   K%=GET:MOVEX%,Y%:PRINT CUR$
1290   IFK%=136THENX%=X%-8
1300   IFK%=137THENX%=X%+8
1310   IFK%=138THENY%=Y%-8
1320   IFK%=139THENY%=Y%+8
1330   MOVEX%,Y%:PRINT CUR$
1340   UNTIL K%>139 OR K%<136
1350 *FX4,0
1360 GCOL0,9:MOVEX%,Y%:PRINT CUR$
1370 VDU4:GCOL0,7
1380 ENDPROC


1390 DEFPROCHEADER
1400 CLS
1410 PRINTTAB(0,0);"Week:    Day:"
1420 PRINTTAB(0,2);"Vibration    Tilt"
1430 ENDPROC


1440 DEFPROCUPDATE
1450 D%=D% MOD 7: D%=D%+1
1460 IF D%=1 THEN W%=W%+1:CLS:PROCGUESS:CLS:PROCH
DER
1470 PRINTTAB(6,0);W%;TAB(14,0);D%;
1480 TILT=RND(35):VIBR=RND(75)
1490 T=EWK-W%+(EDAY-D%)/7
1500 IF T<2 THEN PROCDETECT
1510 PROCMETERS
1520 IF W%=EWK AND D%=EDAY THEN FINISH=TRUE
1530 ENDPROC
```

```
1540 DEFPROCGUESS
1550 COLOUR3:PRINTTAB(0,2);
1560 IF G$="Y"THEN PRINT"Your guess was wrong":SO
UND0,-10,2,15:PROCPLOSTR(GX-16,GY+16,0,"G"):PROCPA
USE(4)
1570 *FX15,1
1580 PRINTTAB(0,2);"Will a volcano eruptnext week
? (Y or N)";
1590 REPEAT G$=GET$
1600   IF G$="Y" OR G$="N" THEN OK=TRUE ELSE OK=F
ALSE:VDU7
1610   UNTIL OK
1620 IFG$="Y" THEN CLS:PROCPUTGUESS
1630 COLOUR 7
1640 ENDPROC


1650 DEFPROCPUTGUESS
1660 PRINTTAB(1,1);"Mark your guess"
1670 PRINT
1680 PRINT"(Use cursor keys andfix guess with any
 other key)"
1690 PROCCURSOR("G")
1700 GX=X%+16:GY=Y%-16
1710 GD%=SQR((EX-GX)^2+(EY-GY)^2)/2
1720 ENDPROC


1730 DEFPROCDETECT
1740 IF TDIST<100 THEN TILT=(2.5-T)*40 ELSE TILT=
RND(50)
1750 IF TILT>96 THEN TILT=96
1760 A%=RND((2.5-T)*80)
1770 VIBR=30*((2.5-T)*20+A%)/SQR(VDIST)
1780 IF VIBR>500 THEN VIBR=250+RND(500)
1790 ENDPROC


1800 DEFPROCMETERS
1810 PRINTTAB(0,3);SPC(99);
1820 GCOL0,5
1830 MOVE700,32:PLOT1,500,TILT
1840 PROCRECT(32,32,VIBR,96)
1850 ENDPROC


1860 DEFPROCFINALE
1870 CLS
1880 PRINT"The eruption was on day ";EDAY;" of we
ek ";EWK
1890 PRINT
1900 IFG$="N"THENS$="You did not predict the erup
tion." ELSE S$="Your guess was "+STR$(GD%)+" kmfro
m the volcano."
1910 PRINT S$
1920 VDU5:GCOL0,9
1930 MOVEEX,EY:VDU42,4:GCOL0,7
1940 ENDPROC


1950 DEFPROCPAUSE(P)
1960 Z%=TIME+P*100
1970 REPEAT: UNTIL TIME>Z%
1980 ENDPROC
```

The Health and Safety Officer of the volcanic island of Disaster
alerts the population to impending doom by issuing newsflashes.
When you have typed the program into the computer and made it
run properly you can invent your own newsflashes.

Newsflash uses many of the procedures in Detect so first you
should load Detect into your computer from cassette. Then do the
following:

1. Type in **DELETE 10,90** and press **RETURN**, then
DELETE 960,1980 and press **RETURN**. This removes the
bits of Detect that are not needed.

2. Type in **RENUMBER 130**. This allows enough room at the
beginning for you to type in a new control routine.

3. Type in the following:

```
  10 MODE2
  20 VDU28,0,31,19,24
  30 PROCISLAND
  40 VDU24,0;250;1279;1023;
  50 PROCSETVOLC
  60 PROCFLASH("ERUPTION STARTS  !!")
  70 IFRND(11)=10THENPROCFLASH("PHEW !!
          WHAT A SCORCHER !!")
  80 PROCERUPT
  90 PROCFLASH("ERUPTION STOPS - NO MOR
E DAMAGE")
 100 PROCPAUSE(7):PROCFLASH("Lava cools
and ash  settles")
 110 VDU19,13,3;0;19,15,7;0;19,5,3;0;17
,7
 120 END


 990 DEFPROCERUPT
1000 DIM NF%(15):FORI%=1TO15:NF%(I%)=0:
NEXT
1010 DIM XA(10),YA(10)
1020 DATA-1,600,900,800,850,920,920,-1,
600,900,800,850,920,820,-1,450,750,400,6
00,175,550,-1
1030 DATA550,750,625,650,600,450,475,38
0,-1,550,750,625,650,600,450,300,400,-1
1040 DATA1100,650,1200,620,-1,920,650,8
20,680,720,550,-1,1000,550,1050,450,900,
400,-2
1050 RESTORE 1020
```

```
1060 VDU19,15,1;0;::VDU19,8,7;0;::VDU19
,10;0;:K%=0:V%=1
1070 REPEAT
1080    READ X%:IFX%<0THEN K%=K%+1
1090    UNTIL K%=P% OR X%=-2
1100 IFX%=-2THENPRINT"PATH NUM. TOO H.
H":STOP
1110 REPEAT
1120    READX%:IFX%>0THENXA(V%)=X%:REAL
A(V%):V%=V%+1
1130    UNTIL X%<0
1140 X1=EX:Y1=EY:K%=0:A=30:B=15
1150 FOR W%=1TOV%-1
1160    X2=XA(W%):Y2=YA(W%):PROCLAVA(2(
:X1=X2:Y1=Y2
1170    NEXT
1180 ENDPROC


1190 DEFPROCLAVA(W)
1200 M%=20:XST=(X2-X1)/M%:YST=(Y2-Y1)/
%
1210 X=X1:Y=Y1:R%=W
1220 FORI%=1TOM%
1230    X=X+XST:Y=Y+YST:R%=R%+RND(W/2)-
/4
1240    IFR%<5THENR%=5
1250    K%=K%+1:IF(K% MOD 4)=1THEN PRO(
SH
1260    GCOL0,15:PROCCIRCLE(X+RND(20)-1
,Y+RND(20)-10,R%)
1270    PROCCHPTS
1280    NEXT
1290 ENDPROC


1300 DEFPROCASH
1310 A=A+20:IFB<70THENB=B+7
1320 GCOL1,5:PROCELLIPSE(A,B,-1)
1330 GCOL0,8:PROCELLIPSE(A,B,0)
1340 ENDPROC


1350 DEFPROCCIRCLE(XC,YC,R)
1360 N%=10
1370 CDEL=COS(2*PI/N%):SDEL=SIN(2*PI/N
)
1380 CTH=1:STH=0:MOVER+XC,YC
1390 FOR J%=1TON%
1400    NCTH=CTH*CDEL-STH*SDEL
1410    NSTH=STH*CDEL+CTH*SDEL
1420    MOVE R*CTH+XC,R*STH+YC:MOVE R*N
TH+XC,R*NSTH+YC
1430    PLOT85,XC,YC
1440    CTH=NCTH:STH=NSTH
1450    NEXT
1460 ENDPROC
```

```
1470 DEFPROCSETVOLC
1480 IFRND(3)=2THENEX=800:EY=500:REG=2
ELSE EX=350:EY=750:REG=1
1490 EX=EX+RND(300):EY=EY+RND(150)
1500 IF REG=1 THEN P%=RND(5) ELSE P%=5+
RND(3)
1510 PHI=-120+RND(120)
1520 ENDPROC


1530 DEFPROCELLIPSE(A,B,FILL)
1540 N%=10
1550 CDEL=COS(2*PI/N%):SDEL=SIN(2*PI/N%
)
1560 CTH=1:STH=0:X%=(A*CTH+SQR(A^2-B^2)
)*COS(RAD(PHI))+EX
1570 Y%=(A*CTH+SQR(A^2-B^2))*SIN(RAD(PH
I))+EY:MOVEX%,Y%
1580 FORJ%=1TON%
1590   XO=X%:YO=Y%
1600   NCTH=CTH*CDEL-STH*SDEL:NSTH=STH*
CDEL+CTH*SDEL
1610   CTH=NCTH:STH=NSTH:XX=A*CTH+SQR(A
^2-B^2):YY=B*STH
1620   X%=XX*COS(RAD(PHI))-YY*SIN(RAD(P
HI))+EX
1630   Y%=XX*SIN(RAD(PHI))+YY*COS(RAD(P
HI))+EY
1640   IF FILL THEN MOVEEX,EY:MOVEXO,YO
:PLOT85,X%,Y% ELSE DRAWX%,Y%
1650   NEXT
1660 ENDPROC


1670 DEFPROCCHPTS
1680 DATA900,900,Lava destroys the    Bu
bblecombe harbour,Dust and ash covers Bu
bblecombe,625,625,Lava destroys bridge -
Ashville cut off,Road temporarily    bl
ocked by ash,500,430,Ashville threatened
by red hot lava," "
1690 DATA320,420,Church and Ashville de
stroyed by lava,Ashville gets a      dust
ing!,1000,500,Lava starts forest  fires,
ash covers forest    killing wildlife and
plants,1080,650,Lava flows towards   Cor
ruption,Dangerous fumes nearCorruption
1700 DATA800,840,Road cut by lava,Ash b
locks road,900,450,Forest fires caused b
y lava,Hot ash kills trees and forest an
imals,750,750,Road cut by lava,Ash block
s road
1710 DATA1140,640,Corruption engulfed-l
ava stops at sea,Suffocating gases    cho
ke Corruption,208,550,Lava flows into se
a - sea boils!," ",-1
1720 RESTORE 1680
1730 F%=0:NOMORE=FALSE
```

```
1740 REPEAT
1750   READX%:IFX%=-1THENNOMORE=TRUE:GO
TO 1800
1760   F%=F%+1:READ Y%,L$,A$:C%=POINT(X
%,Y%)
1770   GCOL3,4:PLOT69,X%,Y%
1780   IFC%=15 AND NF%(F%)MOD10=0 THENP
ROCFLASH(L$):NF%(F%)=NF%(F%)+1
1790   IF(C%=8 OR C%=5) AND NF%(F%)DIV1
0=0 THENPROCFLASH(A$):NF%(F%)=NF%(F%)+10
1800   UNTIL NOMORE
1810 ENDPROC


1820 DEFPROCFLASH(S$)
1830 IFS$=" " THEN GOTO1920
1840 FORS%=1TO5:SOUND1,-10,200,2:SOUND1
,0,200,2:NEXT
1850 COLOUR9:PRINT"+++++++++++++++++++
N E W S   F L A S H !";
1860 COLOUR7:PRINTS$:COLOUR9:PRINT"++++
++++++++++++++++"
1870 PROCPAUSE(3)
1880 ENDPROC


1890 DEFPROCPAUSE(P)
1900 Z%=TIME+P*100
1910 REPEAT :UNTIL TIME>Z%
1920 ENDPROC
```

Disc users please note
If you have disc drives fitted to your computer there will not be enough room in its memory to load and run this program. The best way to overcome this is to split the program into two, calling the first part Map and the second part Newsflash. Here is what you must do:

1. Load Detect into your computer.

2. Type in 40 CHAIN"NEWSFL" and press **RETURN.**

3. Type in **DELETE 960,1980** *and press* **RETURN.**

4. Save this program on disc under the filename **MAP.**

5. Type in **NEW.**

6. Type in the lines of the program opposite. Type in lines 40 to 120 and then lines 990 to 1920. Do not type in lines 10 to 30.

7. Save this program on disc under the filename **NEWSFL.**

Add your own newsflashes
The newsflashes are found as DATA statements in lines 1680 to 1710. Each newsflash has a checkpoint on the map. You can invent different newsflashes to go at the existing checkpoints. If you change the numbers in the DATA statements you will change the positions of the checkpoints. Try experimenting.

Locations and patterns

There are about 500 active volcanoes in the world, including the underwater volcanoes. Most volcanoes occur in strings, rather like beads in a necklace. Many are around the Pacific Ocean forming what is called the 'Pacific Ring of Fire'. Part of this is an area of intense volcanic activity, which occurs in Indonesia, where there are 77 active volcanoes and 90 dormant or extinct ones, more than in any other country in the world.

In comparison, the rest of the world is not very active. There is a broken string through the Mediterranean, and another stretching from the Red Sea down the Great Rift Valley of eastern Africa. But vast areas of Africa, Asia, Europe and the Americas are relatively stable.

Under the surface of the sea, there is another picture. Running north to south down the entire length of the Atlantic Ocean is a vast underwater mountain range called the mid-Atlantic ridge, which is volcanic. It rises above sea level in the north in Iceland where there are a number of active volcanoes, and further south, at several small islands. Similar ridges occur in the Pacific and Indian Oceans. All three ridges are linked together in the south.

There are also deep and surprisingly narrow trenches in the ocean floor. Some circle the Pacific Ocean just inside the Ring of Fire; another trench in the Indian Ocean borders the string of volcanoes in Indonesia.

Clearly there is a pattern to the world map of volcanoes. During the early 1960s, scientists evolved the Plate Theory which describes how volcanoes occur in this pattern.

The Pacific 'Ring of Fire' is clearly seen on this map, which also shows the main volcanic areas and earthquake zones of the world situated along the plate margins. ▶

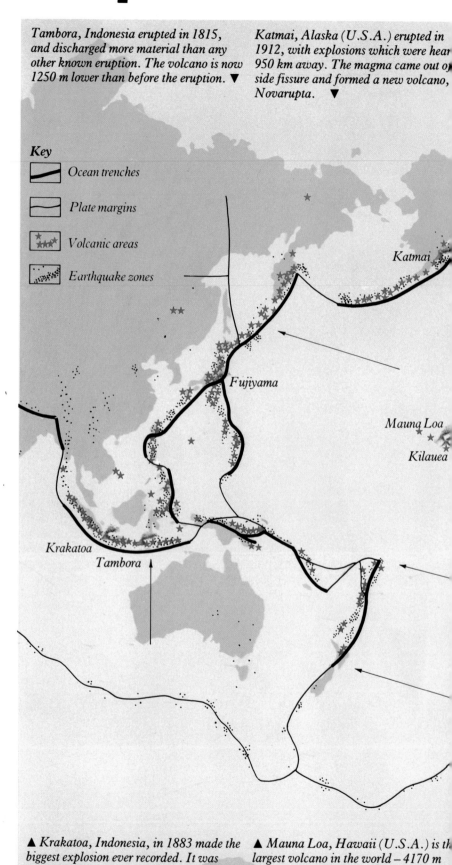

Tambora, Indonesia erupted in 1815, and discharged more material than any other known eruption. The volcano is now 1250 m lower than before the eruption. ▼

Katmai, Alaska (U.S.A.) erupted in 1912, with explosions which were heard 950 km away. The magma came out of side fissure and formed a new volcano, Novarupta. ▼

Key

⎯ Ocean trenches

⎯ Plate margins

★ Volcanic areas

⋯ Earthquake zones

Katmai

Fujiyama

Mauna Loa

Kilauea

Krakatoa

Tambora

▲ *Krakatoa, Indonesia, in 1883 made the biggest explosion ever recorded. It was heard in India and Australia, 5000 km away! It caused a tsunami (giant wave) which drowned 36,000 people.*

▲ *Mauna Loa, Hawaii (U.S.A.) is the largest volcano in the world – 4170 m above sea level, with a base reaching 5180 m below sea level. The base is 120 km across.*

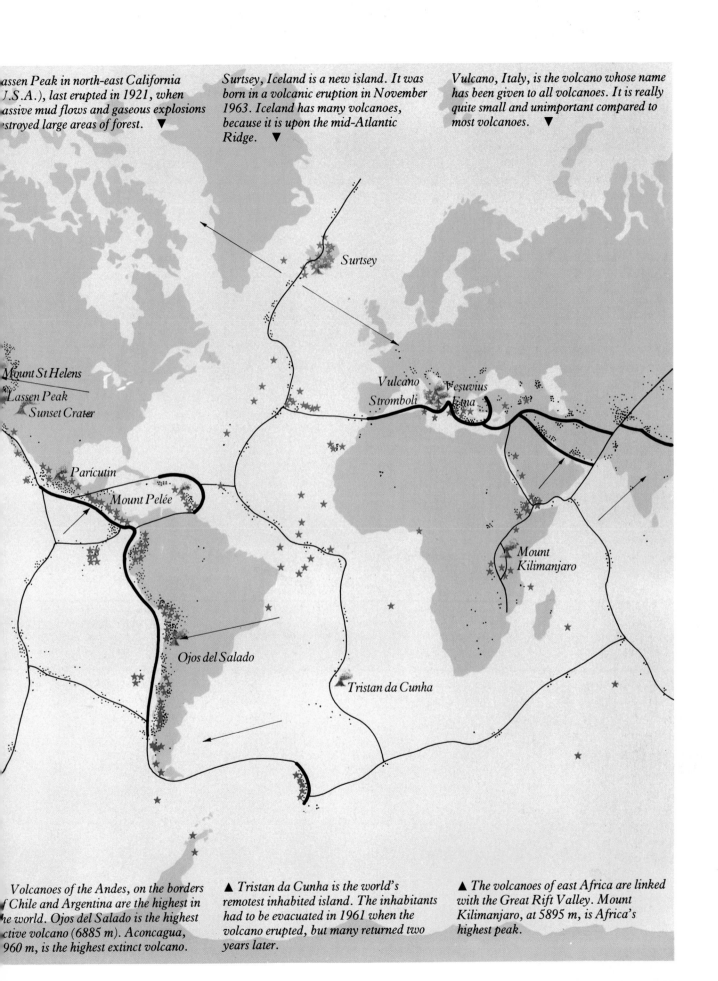

Lassen Peak in north-east California (U.S.A.), last erupted in 1921, when massive mud flows and gaseous explosions destroyed large areas of forest. ▼

Surtsey, Iceland is a new island. It was born in a volcanic eruption in November 1963. Iceland has many volcanoes, because it is upon the mid-Atlantic Ridge. ▼

Vulcano, Italy, is the volcano whose name has been given to all volcanoes. It is really quite small and unimportant compared to most volcanoes. ▼

Surtsey

Mount St Helens
Lassen Peak
Sunset Crater

Vulcano
Stromboli
Vesuvius
Etna

Parícutin
Mount Pelée

Mount Kilimanjaro

Ojos del Salado

Tristan da Cunha

Volcanoes of the Andes, on the borders of Chile and Argentina are the highest in the world. Ojos del Salado is the highest active volcano (6885 m). Aconcagua, 6960 m, is the highest extinct volcano.

▲ Tristan da Cunha is the world's remotest inhabited island. The inhabitants had to be evacuated in 1961 when the volcano erupted, but many returned two years later.

▲ The volcanoes of east Africa are linked with the Great Rift Valley. Mount Kilimanjaro, at 5895 m, is Africa's highest peak.

The plate theory

The earth is a huge ball of rock with a diameter of 13,000 km. In the middle of the ball the rock is white-hot but, because of the immense pressure, it remains solid. About 70 km below the surface of the earth the temperature is just high enough, and the pressure just low enough, for a small amount of the rock to melt slightly, forming a toffee-like layer. We know this layer is there because we can bounce sound waves on it.

The solid surface of the earth forms a sort of mosaic, which moves around very slowly on the toffee-like layer. In some places the mosaic is pulling apart, and new surface is forming in-between the pieces. In other places the pieces of mosaic are pushing together, and one piece is being forced down under the other. Elsewhere pieces are rubbing past each other.

The pieces of the mosaic are called plates and they are very large, some of them are thousands of kilometres across. All is calm in the middle of the plates; it is at the edges, where the plates meet, that the excitement is found. It is at the edges where most of the volcanoes are located.

Volcanoes occur both where the plates are moving apart and where they are pushing together. The plates are moving apart at the mid-ocean ridges. As this happens, magma rises from beneath the earth's crust and forms new plate, and thus new crust and sea floor. Sometimes enough magma comes out to form a new volcano above the sea. This happened in 1963 when the volcano now called Surtsey appeared off the coast of Iceland. The zones where the plates move apart and new crust is constructed are called the

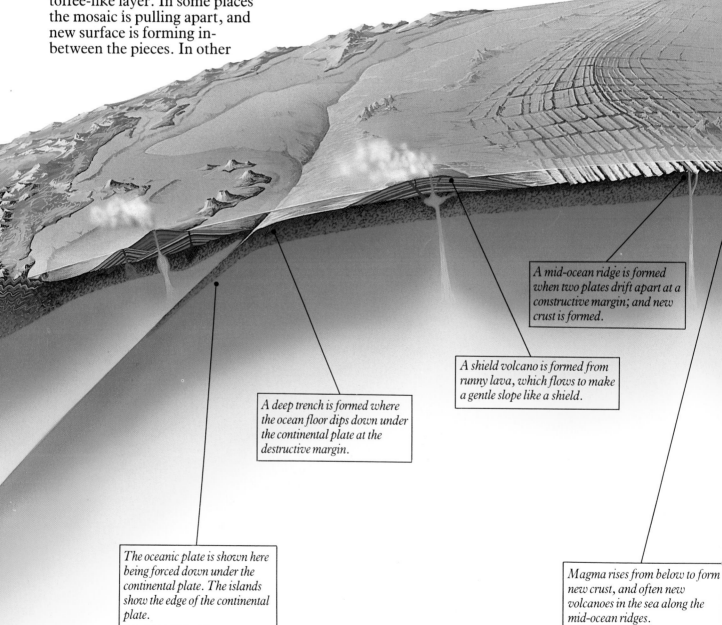

A mid-ocean ridge is formed when two plates drift apart at a constructive margin; and new crust is formed.

A shield volcano is formed from runny lava, which flows to make a gentle slope like a shield.

A deep trench is formed where the ocean floor dips down under the continental plate at the destructive margin.

The oceanic plate is shown here being forced down under the continental plate. The islands show the edge of the continental plate.

Magma rises from below to form new crust, and often new volcanoes in the sea along the mid-ocean ridges.

onstructive margins of the plate.

In other parts of the world, the lates are pushing together. This where there are many arthquakes and volcanoes. The Pacific Ring of Fire' is around he edge of the Pacific Ocean lates. The floor of the Pacific is eing forced down under the mericas (in the east) and under sia (in the west). Where it is orced down, there are deep enches in the ocean floor. On he nearby continents, mountain anges are forced up. Molten material escapes from beneath the earth's crust and erupts on the surface, forming volcanoes. These zones where the plates are pushing together are called destructive margins.

In the Mediterranean, the African plate is slowly moving north and pushing against Europe. Probably the greatest explosion in geologically recent times occurred at this plate margin. Around 1470 B.C. Santorini, in the Aegean Sea, blew up. It is thought that the explosion was over a hundred times greater than the biggest hydrogen bomb tested. The plate margin in the Mediterranean causes the active volcanoes in Italy.

Most volcanoes are formed at the plate margins, but a few are found elsewhere. For example, the volcanoes of the Hawaiian Islands in the mid-Pacific are at a 'hot-spot' in the mantle, which has pierced the plate and has allowed the magma to escape. The Canary Islands were formed over a similar 'hot-spot' in the Atlantic.

The east African volcanoes are close to a rift valley – a place where there are parallel faults in the earth's crust and the land between the faults has slipped down.

Mountains are formed where the earth's surface is pushed and wrinkled up.

A rift valley is formed when there are parallel faults in the earth's crust and the crust sinks between the faults.

The molten rock or magma beneath the earth's crust is at a white hot temperature.

Igneous rock

Igneous rocks are formed from molten magma. Some igneous rocks are intrusive (formed below the earth's surface), and some are extrusive (forming on the surface). They are classified according to their crystalline structure, grain size and texture.

Most rocks with a crystalline structure are igneous. In some rocks, such as granite, the crystals are large and coarse-grained. These were formed by the molten rock cooling slowly, deep within the earth's crust.

Where the crystals are small and fine, these are volcanic rocks, such as basalt, which cooled quickly at or near the earth's surface.

Every town has samples of igneous rock. Speckled granite is very popular for gravestones; old kerbstones are often made from igneous rock. Some old roads have granite 'setts' (square blocks of stone); newer road surfaces may have chippings of igneous rock.

If granite is the local rock, it will be used for building. Many big shops and banks have igneous rocks to make the front of their building look more impressive. You are certain to find granite, but you may find some more unusual rock too.

Look for larvikite from Norway; the crystals glisten with a blue colour and seem to change colour as you walk past. A rough pale green shop front will probably be made from volcanic ash. A patchy dark green and yellow is probably serpentenite, formed deep below the earth's surface.

If you live in lowland areas you will not find big areas of igneous rock. But try looking at the seaside; speckled pebbles on the beach are probably igneous (the crystals make the speckles). And if you live in a glaciated area, you may find similar rocks in the boulder clay that the ice-sheets brought to your garden.

▲ *The pumice mines on Lipari produce a volcanic rock so light that it floats.*

Lava, pumice, obsidian and trachite are all formed as a result of volcanic eruptions. ▼

Pumice

Lava

Trachite

Obsidian

To find out where there are
really large areas of igneous rock,
look at any geological map. The
igneous rocks are usually
coloured red. Most igneous rocks
make high land, but not all high
land is igneous (for example,
Dartmoor is igneous, but
Exmoor is not).

The best basalt in Britain is in
Antrim (Northern Ireland) and
Skye and Mull (Scotland). But
there are smaller areas in unlikely
places. The 'toadstone' in the
Peak District, for example, was
once a lava flow.

▲ *Granite is often used for building. This
cathedral at Santiago de Compostela in
Spain is built of granite.*

*These examples are of the igneous rocks
basalt, andesite and granite.* ▼

Basalt   *Andesite*   *Granite*

This program will test your knowledge of volcanoes. Type the program into your computer, debug it so that it runs properly, and save it on cassette.

The questions and answers are held as DATA statements in lines 10 to 130. Can you invent your own quiz to try on your friends?

```
   10 DATA5,Hot molten rock underground is called
..,Magma,Superheated silica,Lava,Igneous,Basic lav
a
   20 DATA5,What is the name of the volcanic speck
led rock used in building?,Granite,Marble,Sandston
e,Basalt,Pumice
   30 DATA5,The large crater left after a volcano
has exploded is called a ..,Caldera,Fumerole,Cauld
ron,Gulley,Magma chamber
   40 DATA4,Mount Etna is a famous volcano in whic
h country?,Italy,Japan,Mexico,New Zealand
   50 DATA5,Fujiyama is a famous volcano in which
country?,Japan,Italy,Mexico,New Zealand,China
   60 DATA5,Paricutin is a famous volcano in which
 country?,Mexico,Japan,Italy,New Zealand,United St
ates
   70 DATA3,A volcanic plug is ..,rock which sets
hard in the neck of a volcano,something used to st
op an eruption,a pillar of lava pushed up by an er
uption
   80 DATA4,Igneous rocks ..,are formed from magma
,are all formed when a volcano erupts, are made fr
om compressed ash,all contain air bubbles
   90 DATA3,A parasitic cone is ..,a second cone o
n the side of a volcano,the first thing that an er
uption builds,an insect that lives near volcanoes
  100 DATA5,Pumice is a rock type which is ..,Very
 light with many air bubbles,black and shiny (and
igneous),yellow and crumbly,yellow and green (and
igneous),found near hot springs
  110 DATA5,Larvikite is a rock type which is ..,a
n igneous rock with blue crystals,black and shiny
(and igneous),Very light with many air bubbles,yel
low and crumbly,found near hot springs
  120 DATA4,A volcano with steep sides is made fro
m which sort of lava?,Sticky (viscous) lava,Lava w
ith bubbles of gas,Runny (non-viscous) lava,Hot ma
gma
  130 DATA4,A volcano with gentle slopes is made f
rom ...?,Runny (non-viscous) lava,Hot ash and cind
ers,Sticky (viscous) lava,Lava with bubbles of gas
  140 DATA-1
  150 DIM SEQ%(20),ANS$(5)
  160 ENVELOPE1,6,8,0,0,20,0,0,20,-10,-10,-10,126,
0
  170 ENVELOPE2,6,-8,0,0,20,0,0,20,-10,-10,-10,126
,0
  180 TITLE$="V O L C A N O   Q U I Z"
  190 MODE7
  200 *FX4,1
  210 SCORE%=0
  220 PROCFINDNQ
  230 PROCSHUFFLE
  240 PROCQUIZ
  250 PROCPAUSE(3)
  260 CLS:PRINTTAB(0,0)
  270 PROCDBLH(1,3,TITLE$)
  280 PRINTTAB(0,10);
  290 PROCDBLH(7,4,"Your final score was "+STR$(SC
ORE%))
```

```
  300 PRINTTAB(0,12);
  310 PROCDBLH(7,4,"The maximum possible was "+S
$(2*NQ%))
  320 *FX15,1
  330 PRINTTAB(0,20);CHR$(136);CHR$(132);"PRESS
TO REPEAT THE QUIZ"
  340 PRINTCHR$(136);CHR$(132);"PRESS ANY OTHER
Y TO STOP"
  350 IF GET$="R" THEN GOTO 190
  360 CLS:*FX4,0
  370 END


  380 DEFPROCFINDNQ
  390 RESTORE10
  400 NQ%=0:READ N%
  410 REPEAT
  420     NQ%=NQ%+1
  430     FOR I%=1 TO N%+1: READ A$: NEXT
  440     READ N%
  450     UNTIL N%=-1
  460 ENDPROC


  470 DEFPROCSHUFFLE
  480 SEQ%(1)=RND(NQ%)
  490 FOR I%=2 TO NQ%
  500    REPEAT
  510       N%=RND(NQ%): OK=TRUE
  520       FOR J%=1 TO I%-1
  530         IF N%=SEQ%(J%) THEN OK=FALSE
  540         NEXT J%
  550       UNTIL OK
  560     SEQ%(I%)=N%
  570     NEXT I%
  580 ENDPROC


  590 DEFPROCQUIZ
  600 FOR C%=1 TO NQ%
  610    CLS:PROCUPDATE
  620    Q%=SEQ%(C%)
  630    FIRSTGO=TRUE:OK=FALSE
  640    PROCPOSE
  650    REPEAT
  660       CORRECT=FNANSWER
  670       IF CORRECT THEN PROCRIGHT:OK=TRUE ELSE P
ROCWRONG
  680       UNTIL OK
  690    IF C%<>NQ% THEN PRINTTAB(4,9);CHR$(136);
R$(129);"PRESS ANY KEY FOR NEXT QUESTION";TAB(0,
;:K%=GET
  700    NEXT
  710 ENDPROC


  720 DEFPROCPOSE
  730 SOUND1,2,0,12
  740 RESTORE 10
  750 IF Q%=1 THEN GOTO 800
  760 FOR I%=1 TO Q%-1
  770    READ N%
  780    FOR J%=1 TO N%+1: READ A$: NEXT
  790    NEXT
  800 READ N%,QUEST$
  810 FOR I%=1 TO N%: READ ANS$(I%): NEXT
  820 RANS%=RND(N%)
  830 A$=ANS$(RANS%):ANS$(RANS%)=ANS$(1)
  840 ANS$(1)=A$
  850 PRINTTAB(3,11);
  860 PROCLONGSTR(3,39,QUEST$)
  870 FOR L%=1 TO N%
  880    PRINTTAB(0,13+L%*2);
  890    VDU128+L%
  900    PRINTSPC(4);L%;". ";
  910    PROCLONGSTR(8,39,ANS$(L%))
  920    IF LEN(ANS$(L%))>31 THEN PRINTTAB(0,14+L%*
2);:VDU128+L%
  930    NEXT
  940 ENDPROC
```

```
950 DEFFNANSWER
960 *FX15,1
970 PRINTTAB(0,9);CHR$(136);CHR$(130);"SELECT WI
 CURSOR KEYS, THEN RETURN";TAB(0,0)
980 L%=1:PROCHLON
990 FIN=FALSE
000 REPEAT
010   K%=GET
020   IF K%=&8B AND L%>1 THEN PROCHLOFF:L%=L%-1:
OCHLON
030   IF K%=&8A AND L%<N% THEN PROCHLOFF:L%=L%+1
ROCHLON
040   SOUND&11,-10,L%*20,5
050   IF K%=&0D THEN FIN=TRUE
060   UNTIL FIN
070 PRINTTAB(0,9);SPC(40);TAB(0,0)
080 IF L%=RANS% THEN RESULT=TRUE ELSE RESULT=FAL

090 =RESULT


100 DEFPROCHLON
110 PRINTTAB(0,13+L%*2);
120 VDU131,157,132,62,30
130 IF LEN(ANS$(L%))>31 THEN PRINTTAB(0,14+L%*2)
VDU131,157,132,30
140 ENDPROC


150 DEFPROCHLOFF
160 PRINTTAB(0,13+L%*2);
170 VDU128+(L% MOD 7),32,32,32,30
180 IF LEN(ANS$(L%))>31 THEN PRINTTAB(0,14+L%*2)
 VDU128+(L% MOD 7),32,32,30
190 ENDPROC


200 DEFPROCUPDATE
210 PRINTTAB(0,0);
220 PROCDBLH(1,3,TITLE$)
230 PRINTTAB(0,3);
240 PROCDBLH(5,0,"Score: "+STR$(SCORE%)+"      Qu
stion: "+STR$(C%))
250 ENDPROC


1260 DEFPROCRIGHT
1270 IF FIRSTGO THEN SCORE%=SCORE%+2 ELSE SCORE%=
CORE%+1
1280 PROCUPDATE
1290 SOUND&11,1,0,12:SOUND2,2,0,12:SOUND3,1,8,12
1300 PRINTTAB(0,6);
1310 PROCDBLH(1,3,"C O R R E C T !")
1320 ENDPROC


1330 DEFPROCWRONG
1340 PRINTTAB(0,6);
1350 PROCDBLH(5,2,"W R O N G !")
1360 SOUND0,-15,2,16:PROCPAUSE(2)
1370 PROCHLOFF
1380 PRINTTAB(0,6);
1390 IF FIRSTGO THEN PROCDBLH(7,4,"Try again ..")
FIRSTGO=FALSE ELSE PROCDBLH(7,4,"The answer was "
STR$(RANS%)):OK=TRUE:PROCSHOWANS
1400 ENDPROC


1410 DEFPROCDBLH(COL,BKGR,S$)
1420 A%=16-LEN(S$)/2
1430 IF BKGR=0 THEN A%=A%+1
1440 IF A%<0 THEN A%=0
1450 FOR Z%=1 TO 2
1460   IF BKGR<>0 THEN VDU128+BKGR,157
1470   VDU128+COL,141
1480   PRINT SPC(A%);S$;SPC(A%)
1490   NEXT
1500 PRINTTAB(0,0);
1510 ENDPROC
```

```
1520  DEFPROCSHOWANS
1530  SOUND1,-10,L%*20,10:SOUND2,2,L%*20,10:PROCPA
USE(1)
1540  REPEAT
1550    PROCHLOFF
1560    L%=(L% MOD N%)+1
1570    PROCHLON
1580    SOUND1,-10,L%*20,10:SOUND2,2,L%*20,10:PROC
PAUSE(1)
1590    UNTIL L%=RANS%
1600  ENDPROC


1610  DEFPROCPAUSE(P)
1620  Z%=TIME+P*100
1630  REPEAT : UNTIL TIME>Z%
1640  ENDPROC


1650  DEFPROCLONGSTR(LM,RM,Q$)
1660  LSTR=LEN(Q$)
1670  LLENGTH=RM-POS
1680  IF LSTR<=LLENGTH THEN PRINT Q$;:ENDPROC
1690  IF POS<LM THEN PRINT TAB(LM,VPOS);
1700  SPLIT=RM-POS+2
1710  REPEAT
1720    SPLIT=SPLIT-1
1730    UNTIL MID$(Q$,SPLIT,1)=" "
1740  S1$=MID$(Q$,1,SPLIT-1)
1750  S2$=MID$(Q$,SPLIT+1,LSTR-SPLIT)
1760  PRINT S1$;
1770  PRINT TAB(LM,VPOS+1);S2$;
1780  ENDPROC
```

Make up your own quiz

The questions and their answers are stored in DATA statements in lines 10 to 130. Here is an example of a typical DATA statement (but not for a volcano quiz):

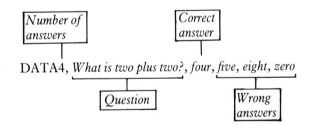

The computer always takes the first answer after the question as the correct answer. Because of this you must be careful when typing in DATA statements. You can make up your own quiz by changing the DATA statements. All you have to do is DELETE the DATA statements in the volcano quiz and replace them by your own. You can have up to twenty questions and each question can have up to five answers. The end of the question is signalled by the DATA−1 statement. This must always be at the end of all the questions.

Last words

Across

1 Hot sticky stuff, from inside the earth (5).
5 You might see a black cloud of this (5).
6 When a volcano comes to life (8).
8 Suoengi, back to front (7).
11 Shiny, black volcanic rock (8).
12 Sweet, sticky seaside stones (5).
14 This mountain destroyed Pompeii (8).
16 This took St Pierre by surprise (5).
18 Many churches are made of this (7).
19 A dead volcano (or is it?) (7).
21 Sticky lava makes this shape (5).
22 The back-bone of Mount Pelée (5).
23 Initially, Look At Volcanoes Around (4).
24 Making electricity from hot rocks and steam (10).

Down

2 Top of a mountain (5).
3 Grey dust (3).
4 A buried Roman city (7).
7 A rock full of holes. You use it in the bath? (6).
9 A hot fountain (6).
10 Volcano with a girl's name (2,6).
12 The opposite of sticky lava (5).
13 A round pyramid (4).
14 Too obvious for words (7).
15 Lava flows out from here (4).
17 A Sicilian volcano (4).
18 It's invisible but it killed St Pierre (3).
20 The hot result of striking a match (4).

Visiting volcanoes

It is possible to visit live volcanoes, and if you have the opportunity, try to join a volcano expedition, but take care. Volcanoes can be dangerous. You should make sure that you are well prepared. You will need a safety helmet with dark goggles to protect your eyes, and boots with strong soles so that you can walk on rough lava. The rest of your clothes should be brightly coloured so that you are easily visible. There will be a lot of heat and dust, so carry plenty of water, and salt tablets to make up for the salt lost by sweating. Finally you should carry a good dressing cream for burns. A burn from hot lava or volcanic gas would be very unpleasant indeed. You might also be planning to camp, in which case you will need warm clothing, food and camping gear.

You may not live near a volcano, but there are places all over the world which you might visit which are volcanic. Iceland has volcanoes, geysers and hot springs. Further south in Italy are Vesuvius and Etna, probably the most visited volcanoes in the world. If you are lucky enough to go to the Pacific, you may be able to visit the volcanoes of Hawaii

Volcanoes can be dangerous and destructive, as is shown in this picture of Heimaey in 1973, when people had to flee their houses to escape the red hot lava, ash and cinders.

However, it is possible to visit a volcano. These people are watching the fountain lava activity in the volcanic crater on Surtsey. ▶

or Indonesia, or the geysers, hot springs and mud pools of New Zealand. The north western area of the United States also has many volcanic features – so enjoy your volcano visiting!

Volcano words

Active A volcano that erupts often or has erupted in recent times.

Ash Particles of *lava*, rock and dust sprayed from the volcano in tiny fragments which fall like ash.

Basalt A dark coloured *igneous* rock made from runny or *non-viscous lava*. It makes a very fine grained rock.

Boiling mud Hot steam and gases from underground make mud on the surface look as though it is boiling.

Boulder clay A thick clay containing rocks and boulders. It is spread over the land by ice sheets during an Ice Age. It makes a fertile soil which is good for farming.

Caldera A large *crater* of over 2 km in diameter left after a volcano has exploded, blowing away the top of the mountain, or in some cases, where the top has collapsed.

Cone A conical hill built by the material thrown out by the volcano.

Constructive margin A boundary of two of the earth's *plates* where they are moving apart and new rock is being made.

Crater The hollow at the top of a volcano left after an eruption has taken place.

Dormant A volcano that has not erupted in recent times. However, it is very difficult to tell whether a volcano is dormant or not and sometimes people can be caught out by a sudden eruption.

Earthquake A sudden movement within the earth's crust which causes shock waves. These make the earth shake and tremble. Earthquake tremors are recorded on a *seismograph*.

Erosion The wearing away of rocks and land by rivers, ice, wind and the sea.

Evaporite deposits These include the deposits of minerals left when hot springs bubble to the surface and the water evaporates. The minerals may be many colours.

Extinct A volcano that is thought to be 'dead'. See also *dormant*.

Fumaroles Holes in the ground near to volcanoes that give off steam and gases. Examples of these can be found in the Valley of Ten Thousand Smokes in Alaska.

Geothermal energy The hot rocks below the earth's surface are used to turn water into steam. The steam turns turbines that make electricity. Geothermal power stations like these are working in a number of places, including Italy and New Zealand.

Glacier A mass of ice which moves slowly downhill along a river valley, making it wider and deeper. If the climate gets warmer, the glacier will gradually melt.

Granite A hard *igneous* rock which has a speckled appearance. It is often used as a building material.

Gully A long 'groove' on a hillside carved out by rainwater running along it.

Gully erosion Hillsides can be worn away or eroded by several gulleys which eat away at the rock. Ash volcanoes are easily eroded in this way.

Hot springs A stream of water that is heated underground and comes to the surface as a hot spring. The Romans used these to heat their public baths, and they are still used today to heat swimming pools, for example the swimming pool at a place called Hot Wells, Bristol, England.

Igenous rocks Rocks that have been made from *magma*. They usually contain crystals that form as the rock cools and sets. *Granite* is an example of an igneous rock.

Larvikite An *igneous rock* from Norway. It has crystals with a blue appearance that can seem to change colour as you walk past.

Lava Molten rock that flows out onto the earth's surface. It cools as it leaves the volcano, and it can make solid rocks of different types. Lava can be *viscous* or *non-viscous*.

Magma Molten rock that forms underground and can force its way to the surface of the earth. Magma becomes *lava* when it reaches the earth's surface.

Mid-ocean ridge A ridge on the sea floor beneath the ocean where the earth's *plates* are being pushed apart. New rock is made along these ridges. The mid-Atlantic ridge is the best known example.

Mud-flow If rainwater mixes with loose ash, a sticky mud is made. This can flow down a volcano very quickly and is very dangerous.

Non-viscous lava This is lava which is thin and runny and usually very hot. It will flow easily and makes wide, flat volcanoes. It has less than 52% of silica, and it can also be called basic lava.

Obsidian A black, shiny *igneous* rock. It can be sharpened to a fine edge and it was used to make tools and weapons centuries ago.

Pacific 'Ring of Fire' A ring of volcanoes that lie along the *plate boundaries* all around the edge of the Pacific Ocean.

Parasitic cone An extra *cone* on a volcano on the side of the main one, for example Vulcanello on the side of Vulcano in the Lipari Islands.

Plates The outer part of the earth's crust is divided up into large pieces of land that move very slowly. Earthquakes and volcanoes often happen near to where these plates move apart or where they meet.

Plug A hard piece of volcanic rock that has set in the neck or *vent* of the volcano. It can act like a cork in a huge bottle of fizzy drink which will explode when the pressure gets too much for it. Sometimes plugs can be all that are left to show where a volcano once stood after the outside has been worn away by *erosion*.

Pluton A large, blob-shaped mass of *igneous rock*. It rises towards the earth's surface as it begins to cool.

Pumice A type of volcanic rock made from *viscous lava* that was full of gas when it was thrown out of the volcano. The lava sets quickly, trapping the gas bubbles inside it. It is a very light rock, and is unusual because it will float on water.

Seismograph A very sensitive instrument that measures and records earth tremors, or vibrations, and the tilt of the land. It is used to predict earthquakes and volcanic eruptions.

Serpentenite An *igneous rock* that is made deep underground. It usually has a dark greenish colour.

Sinter terraces Rock formations made from *evaporite deposits* as the water from hot springs cools and deposits its mineral contents.

Spine A column of solid lava that has been squeezed out of the *vent* like toothpaste, and set hard. Spines are usually worn away quite quickly.

Tsunami A giant sea wave that leads to terrible flooding when it reaches the coast. It is caused by an earthquake on the sea floor or a very large volcanic eruption in the sea.

Vent The mouth of a volcano.

Viscous lava This is lava which is thick and sticky and which does not flow easily. It has more than 52% silica and it is sometimes called acidic lava.

Answers to crossword

	Across		Down
1	Magma	2	Mount
5	Smoke	3	Ash
6	Eruption	4	Pompeii
8	Igneous	7	Pumice
11	Obsidian	9	Geyser
12	Rocks	10	St Helens
14	Vesuvius	12	Runny
16	Pelée	13	Cone
18	Granite	14	Volcano
19	Extinct	15	Vent
21	Steep	17	Etna
22	Spine	18	Gas
23	Lava	20	Fire
24	Geothermal		

Volcano books

Natural Disasters, J. E. Butler, Heinemann Educational, 1976. (Many interesting examples of volcanic eruptions)
Natural Hazards, J. Flatt, Macdonald 'Geography 10-14' Series, 1984. (A text-book with clear and up-to-date explanations)
A Young Person's Guide to Our Planet, Longman, 1980.
Earthquakes, Volcanoes and Mountains, R. Clare, Macdonald Colour Units, 1971. (A colourful and interesting short textbook)
Landforms, I. Galbraith, P. Wiegand, Oxford University Press, 1982. (A very attractive modern textbook)
The Story of Earth, Britain before Man, The Age of the Earth, Volcanoes, all by the Geological Museum, H.M.S.O. (Excellent colour photographs and artwork, with clear explanations)
Planet Earth, a Piccolo Factbook. (Many illustrations and explanations, and highly recommended)
Pompeii, P. Connolly, Macdonald.
Volcanoes, J. Carson, Wayland Planet Earth Series, 1983.
Volcanoes, P. Francis, Pelican, 1976.

Volcano addresses

The Geological Museum, Exhibition Road, London S.W.7.
Italian State Tourist Office, 1 Princes Street, London W.1

Computer words

Introduction

BASIC is the language most commonly used by microcomputers. The word comes from the first letters of the phrase, Beginners All-purpose Symbolic Instruction Code. BASIC is high level language because it uses words similar to human language. Different makes of microcomputer operate different dialects of BASIC. This means that programs written for one make of machine will not always run on another make.

The BASIC language contains commands and statements. These are recognized by the computer because they use special words, called *keywords*. *Commands* are typed in at the keyboard and are obeyed immediately. *Statements* are instructions for the computer that can be stored in the computer's memory in the form of a *program*. They are obeyed when the program is run. A program is a series of lines, each with a line number followed by a BASIC statement. You can have more than one statement on a line if they are separated by a colon (:). When the program is run the statements are obeyed in the same order as the line numbers (although some statements can make the computer repeat or jump over lines in the program).

For the program to do its job properly it must have the right information available, and this information is called *data*. If you wrote a program to draw a straight line between any two points then the computer would have to be given the positions of the start and the end of the line. These two positions would be the data for the program. Either the computer can ask for data with the INPUT statement, or the data could be stored in the program as DATA statements.

After you have typed in a program into the computer's memory you will need some way of keeping it after the power is switched off. This is done by storing the program on to cassette or disc in the form of a *file*. So that you can have more than one program stored on cassette or disc, each file has to be given a *filename* to tell them apart.

Computers can be programmed to do many different tasks. A *database* program is rather like a card index that allows you to store facts about a subject. The facts can be sorted and related to each other, and then printed out, by operating a program which uses the database. For example, a typical database could have the times and places of earthquakes and volcanoes. Using a database program you could find out if earthquakes always happen before a volcanic eruption.

A *simulation* program attempts to show on a computer what happens during a real event. Events in the real world are usually much too complicated for a microcomputer, so computer simulations are simpler than the things they are trying to copy. Think about what happens when a real volcano erupts and compare that with the first program in this book – you will soon see what we mean.

A simulation program often uses *animation*. This is a way of making an object appear to move across the screen by rapidly erasing and then drawing it in a slightly different position. This is just like how cartoon films work. PROCEXPL in the program ERUPT is an example of computer animation.

Commands

SAVE Tells the computer to save the program in the computer on tape or disc. The program must be given a filename of up to 10 characters for tape. The filename must be enclosed in inverted commas. For example, SAVE "ERUPT"

LOAD This is the opposite of SAVE. It will load a program into the computer from either tape or disc. Programs are selected by their filename. For example, LOAD "ERUPT". If you leave out the filename, and just type LOAD "" the next program will be loaded from tape, regardless of its filename.

RUN This tells the computer to start obeying the program stored in its memory.

CHAIN This command first loads a program and then runs it automatically. The program is chosen by its filename. For example, CHAIN "ERUPT". If you just type CHAIN "" the next program on the tape will be loaded and run.

LIST This allows you to look in the computer's memory. If you want to look at the program one part at a time press CTRL and N (at the same time) and then type LIST. You will have to press SHIFT to see the next part of the program. To look at the program between lines 200 and 300 you would have to type LIST 200,300.

RENUMBER This command will renumber your program making the first line 10, the second 20, and so on. RENUMBER 900 will renumber your program starting at line 900.

ELETE You would use this
mmand to delete a line, or
oup of lines, from a program.
or example, DELETE 60,90
ould remove all lines from 60 to
) inclusive.

ariable names

he computer can store numbers
id words in its memory. So that
program doesn't lose track of
erything it has stored it uses
riables. Suppose we wanted to
e a computer to count the
imber of people in a room. We
uld use a variable called
EOPLE, and if there were
even we could put
EOPLE=11. If somebody left
e room we could change the
lue of people:
EOPLE=PEOPLE−1. In this
cample PEOPLE is called a
riable name. If we only want to
ore whole numbers we use the
ecial symbol % at the end of
te variable name:
RUPTIONNUMBER%=2.
o store words we use the special
mbol $ at the end of the
riable name: VOLCANO$=
PARICUTIN" (note how you
ive to put the word in between
verted commas).

ASIC statements

NPUT Way of asking for
formation to be entered whilst
e program is running. For
cample: INPUT "How old are
ou",AGE

RINT Allows the program to
ut messages or the results of
llculations on to the screen. For
cample: PRINT "In ten years
ou will be",AGE+10. PRINT
 itself leaves a blank line.

IOVE Moves the graphics
ırsor to a new position on the
reen without drawing
ıything: MOVE 100,250

DRAW Draws a line from the
position of the graphics cursor to
a new position: DRAW 325,350

COLOUR A statement which
selects the colour for both the
text and its background as
displayed on the screen:
COLOUR 1

GCOL This sets the colour of all
the graphics drawn afterwards in
a program: GCOL 0,2

CLS A statement which clears
the text window. The text
window may not be the same as
the graphics window.

CLG A statement which clears
the graphics window.

DIM Tells the computer to set
up an array. An array is like a
street of numbered houses.
Something can be stored at each
number. For example, in the
program QUIZ we set up an
array with the statement DIM
SEQ%(20) which is used to store
the order that the questions are
asked in.

REM This allows you to put
comments into a program, saying
what it does or how a part of it
works. The computer ignores
everything that appears after a
REM: REM DRAW A LINE.
To save space we have not used
any REMs in the listings in this
book. But if you are writing your
own programs you should use
enough to remind you how it
works.

MODE A statement which
selects the amount of graphics
and text allowed on the screen.

VDU If it is followed by a
number this statement just prints
the corresponding character. But
certain numbers have special
effects. VDU23 is used for user
defined characters. VDU5 writes
text at the graphics cursor, and
VDU4 switches back to writing
text at the text cursor. VDU7
makes a short beep. VDU24
defines the graphics window and
VDU28 the text window.

DEFPROC This marks the start
of procedure definition. The
procedure is given a name which
indicates what it does. The end
of the procedure is marked by
the keyword ENDPROC. For
example, in the program
NEWSFLASH there is a
procedure to draw a filled in
circle: DEFPROCCIRCLE(XC,
YC,R). The position of the
centre of the circle is fixed by XC
and YC, and the circle has a
radius R. Try loading NEWSFL
and then just typing
PROCCIRCLE(300,400,300).

END This keyword tells the
computer that it has reached the
end of the program.

Index

PRINTED IN BELGIUM BY

proost
INTERNATIONAL BOOK PRODUCTI